THE JUDICIARY
IN IRAQ

The Path to an Independent
Judiciary and Modern Court System

Chief Justice Madhat al-Mahmood

*Chief Justice of the Federal Supreme Court of Iraq and
President of the Higher Judicial Council of Iraq*

iUniverse LLC
Bloomington

THE JUDICIARY IN IRAQ

First English Edition 2014
Revised and Expanded from the Second (Arabic) Edition
Edited by William Pryor and Abubakr Zaid

Revised and expanded from the Second Arabic edition with editorial and translation support provided by William Pryor, Abubakr Zaid, and a team of volunteer translators, with special thanks to Husham Abdullah, Dr. Ayad Shams Eldin, Rami Al—Rihani, Hiba, Isaac, and Ahmad.

iUniverse books may be ordered through booksellers or by contacting:

iUniverse LLC
1663 Liberty Drive
Bloomington, IN 47403
www.iuniverse.com
1-800-Authors (1-800-288-4677)

Library of Congress Control Number: 2014907086

ISBN: 978-1-4917-3102-4 (sc)
ISBN: 978-1-4917-3105-5 (hc)
ISBN: 978-1-4917-3114-7 (e)

Printed in the United States of America.

iUniverse rev. date: 06/10/2014

Contents

Part 1
The Historic Foundations of the Modern Judiciary & Courts

Part 2
Growth of the Unique Iraqi system

Part 3
Modern Iraqi Judicial & Court Systems

Part 4
A Personal Note on the Constellation of Martyrs Created
Through the Sacrifice of Iraqi Judges, Court Staff, and Families

Appendices

DEDICATION

To my beloved grandson, Yazin, the son of my martyred son Ahmed; in his eyes I read early maturity and ingenuity. I can see in him and the others of his age all the hope our generations share for Iraq. I write this to help them in their work for Iraq's development and prosperity so that all of Iraq can enjoy security, peace, freedom, dignity, knowledge and all other fruits of a society based on human rights.

This is man's message on earth, which is represented by the development and diffusion of love.

NOTES ON THE FIRST ENGLISH EDITION

This book was originally written in Arabic for a Middle Eastern professional audience that would have an extensive background on Middle Eastern history, jurisprudence, and significant Islamic texts.

Translation of a work that is both technical and deeply personal into a different language and for a wider audience has generated some challenges. The author therefore approved a number of conventions in order to address some of these challenges in this First English Edition:

- In cases where common usage or the lack of an equivalent word makes translation difficult, an Arabic word or phrase may be phonetically rendered in the Latin alphabet, in which case it will be italicized. This compromise often loses the benefits of either extreme option, either full translation or being left in the original alphabet, however the approach follows precedence that has been useful in making concepts accessible to as many non-Arabic speaking readers as possible.

- Transliterated names, however, are not italicized.

- Many different calendars have been used during different periods of Iraq's history, and several are commonly used today. As one theme in this book is the evolution of justice institutions over time, it is important for readers to be able to easily place events on a timeline. This First English Edition adds Gregorian calendar dates or reference points throughout where the original referenced the Islamic or Ottoman calendar. Where non-Gregorian dates are offered, they should be referenced as the more precise if there is any discrepancy.

- The author published portions of this work as part of the proceedings for the Iraqi Judicial Forum, The Judicial System in Iraq: Facts and Prospects, Amman, Jordan, 2-4 October 2004 hosted by UNDP.

- In order to maintain continuity, English translations of the Quran were taken from public domain sources in order to provide widely vetted academic translations with all due respect. The translators kindly refer all questions or suggestions to relevant experts and the original text.

- Many highly valuable sources are only available in Arabic and all citations could not be confirmed in English prior to printing. Where possible within reasonable time frames, the editors located English sources for citations. If this was not possible, the editors and translators attempted to standardize the English translation of names and sources. Readers are in all cases directed to the Arabic source material for further review and consideration.

- Finally, this translation is the product of many different translators who generously volunteered their time in order to provide an English speaking audience a rare view into the perspectives of the Iraqi judiciary. Great effort was invested to standardize English terminology and phrases used within the book, however readers are advised that differences remain between sections. If there is any confusion, please reference the original Arabic version.

In the Name of Allah, the Compassionate, the Merciful.

INTRODUCTION

The word "Iraq" evokes a variety of emotions and thoughts amongst communities around the world. Some reports from the past decade may have left the impression that the modern institutions merged fresh from recent events and significant investments. Iraq, however, is a part of the world that has steadily radiated civilization for ages on end. Regardless of empires expanding, languages changing, and economic forces arising, rectitude—that sense of righteousness underlying many religious, family, and human rights considerations—has managed to prevail through the millennia. History bears witness to the fact that Iraq's inhabitants maintained advanced civilizations dating back to at least 3000 B.C. The people built towns, dug canals and cultivated land as part of a regional economy, feeding themselves and contributing surplus to their neighbors in an active regional economy. The area was critical to the growth of man's greater understanding of religion, and also to man's understanding of how to live together in prosperity and justice.

Modern Iraq evolved from empires that once comprised most of the area now referred to as the Arab Peninsula. Specifically, Iraq is rooted in the empire of Mesopotamia, whose boundaries extended from the Armenian plateau to Shatt-Al-Arab estuary. Iraq is also geographically central to three major religions in the world. The Torah of Judaism, for example, refers to Mesopotamia as the lands of Shinaar, Akkad (covering the northern part), and Sumer (in the south, close to the estuary of the Tigris and Euphrates). Similar references are made throughout both the Old and New Testaments of the Christian Bible, and the more recent advent of Islam is intimately tied with the modern development of Iraq.

The city of Babylon rose to prominence in the 18ᵗʰ century B.C. in a land that was already a rich environment of active people and powerful ideas. Babylon became the center of power as the capital of Mesopotamia when its sixth king, Hammurabi, consolidated the smaller considerations within the lands of Mesopotamia. Hammurabi established a codified set of laws applicable throughout his kingdom more than a thousand years before Roman laws were codified.

People respected the laws of Hammurabi because they safeguarded their rights. People also respected those who administered the law because they were selected for their character and bound by the same laws. Judges are the only public servants addressed directly by the code, which notes that judges are personally liable for bad judgments and can be removed from the bench. Considering the fact that over half of Hammurabi's Code addresses contract and commercial issues, one can presume that the ruler understood that the health of his economy was tied to trust in the rules and in the judges that addressed disputes. Justice was, and is still, the first concern of people seeking to live their lives productively and raise their families safely. In words that resonate in the speeches of many modern leaders and prologues to human rights treaties, Hammurabi declared in the introduction to his code: "I, Hammurabi, the pious prince who fears God, shall try to make justice prevail in the country, destroy the evil and the bad so that the strong will not oppress the weak, and justice shall shine like the sun over people to illuminate the country."[1]

The first people to adjudicate in many societies were priests in places of worship where they administered justice according, mostly, to norms set by the society. In the Arab world before Islam, the clergy, diviners, chieftains and other just men administered justice according to some written or oral laws, customs and, at times, what they considered holy guidance. For example, Sateeh Al-Thunbi, also known as Sateeh the Priest and Shaak Anmaar, considered himself to

---

[1]   Ahmed Zeki Al-Khayyat, *History of Defence in Iraq* (1947), 18.

be the tool of a supernatural power that revealed everything to him. This of course limited options for appeal. The people developed many system of dispute resolution during this period in their thirst for the stability that comes with justice. The formal priests of the time relied on the guidance of one of the many supernatural powers venerated at the time. Another group reached decisions through crafty tools of prognostication. Finally, chieftains, or *sheiks,* also administered or appointed individuals to provide justice using the more secular tools of logic and custom. When anyone in a tribe showed exceptional intellectual ability and acumen, he would take over adjudication in the tribe. The ancestors of the Prophet, may peace be upon Him, included famous tribal adjudicators such as Hashin bin Abul Munaaf and Abu Talib from the Kurayish tribe. Among the well-known tribal judges of that period were Amer bin Al-Tharib and Akkitham bin Sayfi, the famous "judicious Arab" who was regarded as the best judge of his time.[2]

It has taken many centuries for a class of professionals to evolve separately from the tribal leaders, rulers and priests to administer justice based on rules and principles. These professionals have become the judiciary of today. While judges are selected and governed by many different systems around the world, the judiciary as a class enjoy the esteem of people because of the burden it carries in keeping social balance. In contrast to other elements in society that may feel obligated to push for agendas or individual gain, history shows that the role of the judiciary specifically grew to counterbalance the expected bias of the powerful. Judges were charged with reclaiming the rights of the abused from those who usurped them and returning peace to the troubled in a manner that earned the trust of the population. Without trust in the adjudicators, the people, whether Arab or not, will rely on violence or other disruptive means to resolve disputes. The pre-cursors of the judiciary in the Arab world, with Iraq

---

[2]   Ismael Hakki Faraj, *Islamic Judiciary and Its History* (Ibrahim Al-Waeth,1948); Mohammed Shaheer Arslaan, *Judiciary and Judges* (King Fahad Press, 1969), 49.

at the center as the birthplace of codes such as that of Hammuabi, have shouldered the burden of bringing justice to people for more than three thousand years. The systems that govern the profession have been forged in many trials over the centuries. At their best, the systems have maintained a focus on the rights of all in spite of the vagaries of political and economic contests.

It is worth mentioning that most of the Arabs before Islam had wandered from the system of Hammurabi. They also did not yet know of a legislative power that separated the creation of laws from the executive power of enforcement in the modern sense of governance. For most, then, a *sheik* was the head of the tribe that made and enforced rules as well as adjudicated based on norms, traditions, experience, beliefs, and precedents. This was also the case with tribes and communities neighboring and living within the Arab civilizations, such as the Persians, Romans, Jews, and Christians. Common usage and understanding made norms and traditions unwritten legal provisions, however the role of adjudicators became advisory. In the pre-Islamic era an aggrieved party could seek adjudication as a matter of choice without being bound to follow the final decision. Both parties could either go to another judge or refuse to implement the order altogether.[3]

With the arrival of Islam different definitions of words related to the English word "judge" evolved. More nuanced forms of the nouns and verbs related to the root evolve because the Quran uses related words in a variety of contexts. For example, the root of "judge" is made into both a noun and verb in the following passage to mean both the act of making a decision and the person that makes the decision: "Give your judgment in what you are a judge"[4]; a similar root is used in

---

[3]   Mohammed Shaher Arslaan, *Judiciary and Judges*, 10.

[4]   The Holy Qur'an. Surah Ta Ha, 20:72, Trans. M.H. Shakir. Tahrike Tarsile Qur'an, Inc., 1983. http://quod.lib.umich.edu/cgi/k/koran/koran-idx?type=DIV0&byte=480576, accessed 20 August 2011.

the sense of *accomplishing or completing something* as in "when Zaid had accomplished her"[5]; a third variation arises from the root to mean *proclaiming* or *decreeing* as in "He ordained them seven heavens in two periods".[6]

Linguistically, in Arabic some dictionaries define the word for *judiciary* as judgment or decision based on the word "*qadhaytu*", meaning "I decided". Thus we say in Arabic "*istaqadha Fulan*" meaning "He decided to appoint Fulan as a judge". In idiomatic usage, Ibn Khaldun (died in 808AH-1405AD) further expands the meaning of *qadha*, which is a noun based on the same root as *qadhaytu*, as "[t]he post responsible for addressing disputes between people in order to prevent deterioration of peace, using legal judgment and based on the Quran and the traditions of the Prophet Mohammed and the wise caliphs after him. It is one of the posts beholden to the caliph."[7] From this example, we can say that the Arab world had evolved away from the advisory, or optional, opinion.[8]

Under Islam, the judgment of a *qadha* became an order that must be followed, issued by someone empowered with a general jurisdiction, as captured in the following verse: "But no, by the Lord, they can have no (real) Faith until they make thee judge in all disputes between them, and find in their souls no resistance against Thy

5 The Holy Qur'an. Surah Al-Ahzaab, 33:37, Trans. M.H. Shakir. Tahrike Tarsile Qur'an, Inc., 1983. http://quod.lib.umich.edu/cgi/k/koran/koran-idx?type=DIV0&byte=650389, accessed 20 August 2011.

6 The Holy Qur'an. Surah Ha Mim, 41:12, Trans. M.H. Shakir. Tahrike Tarsile Qur'an, Inc., 1983. http://quod.lib.umich.edu/cgi/k/koran/koran-idx?type=DIV0&byte=747753, accessed 20 August 2011.

7 Ibn Khaldun, *An Introduction* (Beirut: Jamal Establishment for Printing and Publishing, Beirut, 1975), 77.

8 Mohammed Shaher Arslaan, *Judiciary and Judges*, 10.

decisions, but accept them with the fullest conviction."[9] Today we use similar language, saying "a judge has decided", meaning he has accorded a right to a party that is deemed its rightful owner.

Islam defined many new roles directly and indirectly. By establishing formal posts, affirming the binding nature of decisions, and through the many examples of the importance of the role of judges in pursuing justice in the Quran, the new religion gave the judiciary a higher status than it had before Islam. At the most fundamental level, the Quran demonstrates that giving judgment is a responsibility that God reserved only for the most respected; in the beginning the Prophet Mohammed himself administered the law. In other examples, the Quran says "judgment is only for God"[10] and, with regard to David, "O, David, We have made you a ruler in the land, so judge between men with justice and do not follow desire lest it should lead you astray from the path of God."[11] It would not be fair to hold today's humble judiciary to the holy example set by the Prophet Mohammed when he became a judge on orders from the Almighty God. We must instead be inspired by the Prophet's example, which shows the importance of judges to a peaceful society, and aspire to perform to the best of the abilities He has given us: "so judge thou between men in truth (and justice): Nor follow thou the [wishes of men], for they will mislead thee from the Path of Allah"[12]

---

[9]   The Holy Qur'an. Surah An Nisaa, 4:65, Trans. Quran Database. http://www.oneummah.net/quran/book/4.html, accessed 20 August 2011.

[10]   The Holy Qur'an. Surah Yusuf, 12:40, 12:67, Trans. M.H. Shakir. Tahrike Tarsile Qur'an, Inc., 1983. http://quod.lib.umich.edu/cgi/k/koran/koran-idx?type=DIV0&byte=356419, accessed 20 August 2011.

[11]   The Holy Qur'an. Surah Suad, 38:26, Trans. M.H. Shakir. Tahrike Tarsile Qur'an, Inc., 1983. http://quod.lib.umich.edu/cgi/k/koran/koran-idx?type=DIV0&byte=708759, accessed 20 August 2011.

[12]   The Holy Qur'an. Saad Surat, 38:26, Trans. Quran Database. http://www.oneummah.net/quran/book/38.html, accessed 27 December 2013.

In the time of the Prophet Mohammed, the position of judge was allocated to a small, select group of people in the nation. Two of the earliest judges were Caliph Omar bin Al-Khattab and Ali bin Abi Talib, whom the Prophet warmly referred to as *Al-Shabah,* the Companion, and history sometimes records as Abu Al-Hassan, which means "the father of Hassan." Caliph Omar bin Al-Khattab himself disliked adjudicating in a critical case when Ali bin Abi Talib was not also present. Because of the high rank associated with the position of *qadha* (judge) under Islam, it was originally accorded only to caliphs. Each caliph performed what today would be considered executive and legislative responsibilities as part of their defined role and also held the additional post of *qadha*. But with the expansion of Islam far and wide, the number and diversity of cases increased. The need arose for rapid, just solutions to disagreements in order to maintain peace between peoples from many different backgrounds and religions. As demonstrated by the guidance given to David in the Quran, Islam obliges leaders, and by extension the state, to provide justice for all. Over time, therefore, caliphs began appointing judges in their territories that could focus solely on resolving disputes while the caliph concentrated more on executive functions.

More than a millennia ago, adjudication in the Arab world was entrusted to specialized jurists because the caliph was not able to manage the growing number of complex cases along with other increasing obligations. Within a few centuries of the time of the Prophet, we find precursors to the modern framework where the judicial authority was separated from the general executive and rule making authority. Caliph Omar bin Al-Khattab is regarded as the first to separate the judiciary from the executive power when he appointed Abu Al-Darda as a judge in Al-Madina, Sharih a judge in Basra, and Abu Musa Al-Aharee as a judge in Kufa. We now realize that these were the first professional judges in the Islamic world.[13] Leaders were eager to support the new judges with resources because of the difficulties of the position (as the caliphs themselves experienced when they tried to perform the duties as part of their own work). The level of support further illustrates the rank and status of the judge in the Arabic world under Islam, which by this time already encompassed lands with many different ethnic and religious groups.[14]

Over the next few centuries the position of judges continued to evolve in the Islamic world. In the Prudent Caliphs Era (11-39 AH/ 632-659 AD), the religious teachings calling for toleration and Islamic values persisted among the people and were reflected in their deeds

---

[13]   Sahih al-Bukhari, Vol 4, p 1628. [Editor's Note: a hard copy of this religious work was not available to confirm volume and page references. Readers are directed to http://www.usc.edu/org/cmje/religious-texts/ hadith/bukhari/ for a translation. Accessed 25 February 2014.].

[14]   Mohammed Shaher Arslaan, Judiciary and Judges, 55; Othmaan Shawakit, Adjudicating for the Oppressed, 26. Caliph Omar bin Al-Khattab, after appointing Abi Mussa Al-Asharee as a judge in Basrah, wrote to him: "Treat people equally—in your look, adjudication, and chamber so that a nobleman does not devour you and a poor one does not lose hope in your justice." Al-Marudi, The Literature of Judges, Part One, 134. In the same vein, Ali bin Abi Talib, after appointing Al-Ashter Al-Nakhee as a governor in Egypt wrote to him, "For the post of a judge, select one from those closest to you who is well to do and whom opponents cannot swerve from a straight line, who does not indulge in wrong-doing, does not hesitate from joining the right when he knows it, does not have any liking for avarice, does not remain content with the minimum understanding, whose suspicion comes true, who accepts proofs, does not get bored when a litigant presses his/ her claim but waits until things clear up, words his judgment clearly, does not like being praised and is not lured - and there are few like him. Support him very often. Give him handsome remuneration, thus increasing his integrity and keeping him from asking support from other people. Give him of your time that none of your retinue will envy him thus he is not afraid that people will slander him in front of you. Look into this carefully." Al-Ashmawi, Procedural Rules in Egyptian Judiciary, Part One (Al-Namuthajeha Press), 24.

and obligations. Many disputes were resolved either by reconciliation or through acceptance of judgment. The litigants were satisfied with the judgment passed by the judges who were either jurists or the Prophet Mohammed's companions, indicating Islamic teachings were deeply held and adhered to. In the Umayyid Era (41-132 AH/661-849AD) many *Diwans,* or local dispute resolution offices, to address complaints, were set up. In just a few decades the power to judge had devolved from the caliph down to trusted judges that could manage independent *Diwans* to adjudicate disputes in places easily accessible to the population. The caliphs did not interfere in judicial business and the judges themselves ensured that they did not interfere in caliphate business. Early judges were responsible for all types of disputes, both civil and religious, so they adjudicated according to their prudence, the Quran, and the teaching of Prophet Mohammed and his companions. By around 100 AH / 720 AD, judges had become one of the foundations of the governance structure, the most important of the "several pillars" that support a governor's rule.

Throughout this period, individual judges began to rise to prominence, providing additional respect for the office and guidance to other judges. Several examples are Al-Hassan Al-Basri (21-110 Ah/641-719 AD), a trustworthy jurist in Basra during the reign of Caliph Omer bin Abdul Aziz. Another prominent judge was Judge Shreeh (died in 82 AH/ 701 AD), who held the post of judge in Kufa for 75 years until he was dismissed by Al-Hajaj bin Yousif Al,Thakafiy.[15] Stanley Linpaul wrote that by the time Europe was reaching the Middle Ages, the position of judge in Egypt had become a professional post: "A judge in Egypt during Umayyid Era and early Abbasseen Era enjoyed an important position, had great influence, and kept his post although governors were replaced. He did not hesitate to submit his resignation if anybody interfered in his decision. He gained good reputation for rectitude and good manners that governors always hesitated before deciding on

---

[15]   Hassan Ibrahim, Dr., and Ali Ibrahim, *The Islamic System*, 345, quoting Mohammed Shaher Arslaan, *Judiciary and Judges*, 142.

dismissing a judge lest they antagonize the people. Moreover only a caliph could dismiss a judge at that time."[16]

In the first Abbassid era (750-1258 AD) the position of judge and role of the judiciary became more clear. The status of judges became more defined, and the role of judges expanded to include addressing problems with even senior ministers and interpreting Sharia law. The judge was no longer under the authority of governors in areas where they were posted. The judge was appointed directly by the Abassid caliph in Baghdad, who supported the judiciary and judicial institutions to the point of bestowing a holy character to their judgments. History books speak of judges' integrity, rectitude, and commitment. For the sake of the right, they never paid attention to criticism. During this period, judges were appointed and dismissed only by the central authority which also oversaw their judgments through what the Special Correspondence Director submitted to the caliph. By this point, the role of the judiciary had become so trusted that a number of ministers and top officials were brought to trial when they failed to carry out their obligations toward the people.

In practice, the functional necessity of having societal access to trusted systems for dispute resolution meant that caliphs continued appointing judges even in periods when the caliph's authority was shaken or when there was political instability. At this point of development, a judge maintained both religious and civic responsibilities. While the caliph appointed judges, the judges maintained the responsibility for interpreting the *Shari'a* from which the caliph derived their legitimacy. Moreover, the jurisdiction of the judge was expanded. He could now rule in matters related to real estate and family matters. For these reasons, the Abbassid Era is considered an historical golden age for the development of judicial and Islamic legislative frameworks. The period saw the establishment

---

[16] Abdul Razzak al-Anbari, *The Post of a Chief Judge during the Abassid Time*, (Beirut: Arab House for Encyclopedias, 1987), 101.

of the post of Chief Justice and the addition of judges to diversify Islamic theological jurisprudence. Furthermore, caliphs encouraged the work of *Al-Fuqaha*, religious scholars, in researching the role of justice in various aspects of life in the expanding Islamic state.

It is interesting to consider that the role of the judiciary grew long before the idea of a dedicated place for hearing cases took root. As a matter of practice, there was no fixed place to hold hearings and administer the judicial system in the olden days. It was common for a judge to sit in a mosque, which was then, as now, a public facility used for various activities in addition to worshipping. As cases became more querulous, the raised voices and noise became incompatible with the high position a mosque has in Islam.[17]

We have walked quickly through the development of the judiciary in the Arab world. I see similarities in the development of professional classes dedicated to justice in other nations through, for example, constitutions that sincerely reflect the nations' conscience and beliefs. These constitutions regard the judiciary highly and show the nearly global belief that judicial independence is fundamental to the existence of the state itself as well as to the freedom of its citizens. Iraq, even under the Ottomans' rule, remained faithful to the judiciary, giving it the same status it enjoyed before the advent of Islam. I believe that looking at the role of the judiciary in the recent history of Iraq, starting from the Ottoman Era and moving through the British occupation and setting up of the modern Iraqi state in its various phases, will guide our consideration of what role the judiciary can play today so that justice predominates.

Since the earlier editions of this book, many developments have taken place in the Iraqi judicial system, creating an urgent need to enlarge some chapters and record the resulting developments so that research in law will be served. I mention with a heavy heart that the number

---

[17]   al-Anbari, *The Post of a Chief Judge during the Abassid Time*, 73.

of martyrs taken from the ranks of judges, court administrators, and staff has also grown. The people of Iraq may never realize who has given their life for them, however the spirit of justice grows in spite of challenges because of their sacrifice.

This is the aim of the present modest study. I would like to thank Judge Zuhair Kadhim Abood, Judicial Supervisor, for his part in editing the book. It honors me to lay a small brick to raise the tower of justice. With the help from God we succeed.

Chief Justice Medhat Al-Mahmud
January 10, 2010
Baghdad

Addendum: The Passage of Law No. 112 of 2012

The Iraqi Council of Representatives, in its session of 15 December 2012, promulgated Law No. 112 of 2012 on the Higher Judicial Council and sent it to the President's Office for approval. The law was considered approved based upon the lapse of 15 days from the date on which it was received pursuant to article 73 (3) of the Constitution. The law was published in the Official Gazette, issue 4266, on 4 February 2013.

Law No. 112 has a complicated past that was further confused by the delayed implementation of the 2005 Constitution that several academics have discussed at length from a variety or perspectives.[18] Originally prepared as a draft for discussion by several civil society organizations in cooperation with some international institutions, the draft that eventually became Law No. 112 was circulated for several years without the participation of the Judicial Council that was formed under Order No. 35 of 2003 and then duly empowered under the

---

[18] *Musings on Iraq Blog;* "How Faults with Iraq's Constitution Undermines the Country, Interview with Constitutional Scholar Zaid Al-Ali," blog entry by Joel Wing, 24 February 2014.

2005 Constitution to manage the affairs of the newly independent judiciary. The civil society draft was submitted to the Presidency Council's Office at some point through an unknown mechanism.[19] In 2007, the Presidency Council's Office sent the civil society draft to the Council of Representatives. There was no action taken on the law at that time because the Higher Judicial Council was preparing a consolidated draft law to regulate the activity of the judiciary and courts as mandated under Article 89 of the Constitution. Article 89 states that "the federal judicial authority shall comprise a Higher Judicial Council, Federal Supreme Court, Federal Court of Cassation, Public Prosecution Agency, Judiciary Oversight Commission, and other federal courts that are regulated according to the law."

When the Higher Judicial Council learned that the civil society draft law had been submitted to the Council of Representatives, it notified the Secretariat General of the Council of Ministers and requested that the Council of Representatives return the draft law so that it could be considered as part of the resource material for the more comprehensive consolidated law being drafted for the judicial authority and courts. Parts of the civil society law dated from before the passage of the 2005 Constitution and were inconsistent with the Constitution and other provisions. The Council of Representatives refused to return the draft law at the time due to political pressures, and certain blocks made substantive changes to the draft. Demonstrating the significant gap in the procedures governing the drafting of organic legislation, the

---

[19] Editor's Note: in the confusion of 2005, several important aspects about who can draft and submit laws through various mechanisms were not addressed in the final Constitution. The path for a law drafted by the Higher Judicial Council to be considered by Parliament, for example, was deemed murky by some academics after the HJC was separated from the MoJ (See, for example, the work of the Global Justice Project Iraq, which drafted proposed amendments to the Criminal Procedure Law through funding from the US Department of State / INL. http://gjpi.org/ Accessed 26 February 2014). In light of this, laws generated by external bodies, such as civil society, were also not easily inserted into the drafting process using defined pathways.

considerations of the judicary and the wider public were never taken into account during the drafting and revision of the civil society draft, which ultimately spanned nearly 7 years from drafting to promulgation.

In pursuing narrow personal and political aims, the new law deflates fundamental structures established in furtherance of the Constitution itself. For example, Law No. 112 considers the Higher Judicial Council an administrative body that administers the affairs of the judicial bodies even though the Constitution affirmed its role as a fundamental part of the judicial authority. Law No. 112 also stipulates that the president of the Higher Judicial Council shall be the chief justice of the Federal Court of Cassation instead of the chief justice of the Federal Supreme Court as the Constitution was interpreted in 2005. Two cases outlining reasons why this law is unconstitutional were submitted in 2013 and are expected to be heard by the Federal Supreme Court imminently.

[Editor's Note: In September 2013, Madhat al-Mahmood was reinstated as the President of the Higher Judicial Council and Chief Justice of the Federal Supreme Court when Law No. 112 of 2012 was declared unconstitutional.[20]]

---

20   *Shafaq News*; "Federal Court Returns Medhat Mahmoud as Head of the Supreme Judicial Council," entry posted 16 September 2013.

PART 1

The Historic Foundations of the Modern Judiciary & Courts

CHAPTER ONE

The Arrival of Civil Law Structures Under the Ottoman Empire

We discuss in the introduction the development of the judiciary in Iraq from the pre-Islamic to the Islamic state.

In this overview of the judicial system in Iraq, we are turning to more modern developments, and need to look more specifically at the impact of Iraq's time as part of the Ottoman Empire. There were large scale social and cultural impacts of Ottoman rule on Iraq, however in the context of the current discussion I am focusing on three general themes initiated by the Ottomans that significantly impacted the modern legal environment in Iraq. First, the Ottomans created a professional class of judges by establishing formal, objective requirements for people appointed as judges. Second, the Ottomans codified laws built from *Sharia* foundations and based on the Ottoman's exposure to French systems. Third, court structures and procedural rules evolved under the Ottomans into shapes recognizable to modern Iraqis as early as the beginning of the 20th century.

The Ottomans occupied Iraq from 1532 to 1918 when the British completed the takeover they began in Basrah in 1914. For political and administrative purposes, Iraq was divided into three primary *wilayah,* or provinces, Mosul, Baghdad, and Basrah, which included the historic areas of Sharazur to the east of the Tigris River and Al-Hassa on the west coast of the Persian Gulf. Ottoman administration in Iraq changed over the centuries to reflect the priorities of various rulers at different points. The early highly centralized rule of the Ottomans gave way to semi-autonomous structures by the seventeenth and eighteenth centuries, albeit with Ottomon governors. The Ottomons returned to direct central control over Iraqi provinces in the nineteenth century.

The Ottomans divided their administrative framework into three primary commissions:

1. The Academic Commission;

2. The Pen Commission; and

3. The Military Commission.

The Academic Commission addressed the needs of the Islamic religious institutions covering the principle religious men and religious (Sharia), including religious education, religious schools themselves, the affairs of religious courts, endowments, and so on. The Academic Commission was presided over by a *Sheikh al Islam*, or Chief Theologian, who chaired the Commission and was at the same time the prime authority for judges. The central Ottoman state appointed judges in occupied areas in an attempt to ensure a uniform application of justice and thereby provide security. The judiciary in the Ottomans state was Islamic oriented just as other institutions of the times. It also had unique and independent characteristics. As the tumultuous events pressured the Ottoman state, the framework for the judiciary was amended several times through decrees of the Sultans. Ultimately, the central authority responsible for the judiciary was divided into three branches:

1. The Roman judiciary;

2. The Antalya judiciary to which the judiciary of the Arab territories and the judiciary of Iranians were added; and

3. The Egyptian military judiciary.

The judges in the territories of what is now Europe were beholden to the judge within the Roman branch, the Antalya and Arab territory judges to the Antalya branch, and the Egyptian judges to the last branch. The title of "Judge of the Military" is equivalent to Chief Justice within the traditions of the Islamic judiciary, however the position also maintained a distinct responsibility for the religious affairs of the military. The Judge of the Military accompanied the Sultan and his army during their invasions, and would also perform as the second chairman of the Academic Commission in the Ottoman state and participate in the sessions of the Ottoman State Council. The Military Justice submitted applications of candidates for the post of judge for the Sultan's consideration until 1574 when the Sheikh of Islam took over this responsibility. After 1574 the Military Justice still appointed judges and teachers within his region of responsibility.[21]

During most of the Ottoman rule, Iraq, with its three *wilayahs,* knew only one type of court. All cases were heard by religious courts that based their judgments on *Sharia* law and related religious edicts. The Sultan in Istanbul, which remained the capital, appointed judges to these courts by a decree called the *Sharifiya* Certificate; the Sultan was the only one who could dismiss a judge once they were appointed. A body of laws and regulations governing the judiciary began to grow under the Ottomans. The scope and depth of laws passed by the Ottomans demonstrate the investment in courts and judges during the period. In a brief span of time, the following laws were published:

• Regulations on selecting a judge issued on 11.4.1329

• Judges Law issued on 13.12.1329 and its amendment

[21]   Ismail Ahmed Yaghi, *The Ottomans State in the Modern Islamic History*, (Al-Ubaykaat Bookstore, 1996), 89.

- The Characteristics of Legal Arbitrators and Judges issued on 17.5.1320

- The Characteristics of Legal Arbitrators issued on 17.5.1320

In particular, the laws created standard requirements for candidates for the post of a judge, a major step forward in creating an objective professional class. For example, the regulations established the following requirements for candidates:

- Must be at least 25 years of age;

- Candidate must not be covered by any other legal provision that bars him from taking up the post of a judge;

- Candidate must not have been sentenced for more than a week for an ordinary crime;

- Candidate must satisfy the terms stipulated in Articles 1729 and 1994 of the *Mecelle* , discussed in more detail below, which state:

  1- Person must show sound judgment, be a model of rectitude, honesty, and religion. A minor, an idiot, a blind, or a deaf person shall not be a member of the judiciary.

  2- Person must have qualifications from a law school or passed examinations in the subjects taught at such a school.

On meeting these requirements, he would be appointed a judge after the issuance of a *Sharifiya* Certificate pursuant to provisions of Article 18 of the Ottomans Fundamental Law.[22]

By the start of the 19th Century, judges carried out the hearings and handed out judgments according to procedures recognizable to practitioners using the current civil and penal procedures in Iraq. A single type of court still heard all cases, including family, business and *Sharia* cases, until 1856 when Sultan Abdul Majeed issued an Order that reformed the Ottoman government structure and adopted some Western laws. The reforms of 1856 were expanded in 1880 under the reign of Sultan Abdul Hameed the Second, and the *wilayahs* of Iraq saw formal courts established for the first time. These new courts primarily addressed criminal cases and cases related to the ownership of land.

The additional courts in Iraq were established in parallel with administrative units in place at the time. From smallest unit to largest, the courts started with the village, the *Nahiya*, the *Kadaah*, and then the *Liwa* at the provincial level.[23] In order for the ordinary citizen to file a lawsuit easily, courts called *Al-Sulih*, Reconciliation Offices, were set up in *Nahiyas* and *Kadaahs* to resolve disputes. They were run by members of the village council and village chieftain's council. The jurisdiction of these courts covered members of the village, or *Al-Nahiya*. The *Al-Sulih*, or Reconciliation, Law of 1913 established accessible courts in every *Nahiya* center that could be moved to subordinate villages as the need arose. These mobile courts were intended to create accessible access to state justice throughout rural Iraq nearly a century ago. As a matter of practice, *Al-Sulih* were set up only in some important *Nahiya* centers staffed with a judge

---

[22] Abdul Hameed Kuba, *Judicial Organizations and Legislative Movement in Iraq*, 160.

[23] Abdul Rahmaan Kedur. "Judicial Development in Iraq." *Judicial Journal*, Vol 1 (1937): 37.

assisted by a certain number of officials who were authorized to hear cases when the judge was absent.[24]

The Ottomans established First Instance Courts consisting of a presiding judge and two members in *Kadaa* and province centers. These courts carried out the task of *Al-Sulih* as well as hearing cases and investigating crimes committed in the geographic areas. After completing the investigation the First Instance Court referred them to high criminal courts.[25] The First Instance Court in Baghdad enjoyed special importance in view of the importance of Baghdad among other Iraqi cities. This court consisted of two separate commissions: one for civil lawsuits and another for business cases.[26]

In addition to Personal Status Courts, *Al-Sulih* Courts and First Instance Courts, the Ottomans established Courts of Appeal in the *Kadaa* centers. A Court of Appeal was made up of a Chief Justice and four other judges. Its function was to look into appeals against judgments in civil and business cases from the Courts of First Instance within the *wilayah*.[27] Finally, a Court of Cassation headquartered in Istanbul would monitor the judgments passed by courts throughout the Ottoman Empire.

In another trend, the new courts had new laws to apply, including some that Ottoman legislators adopted from the West such as the Ottoman Penal Code. Most of the new provisions were taken from French legislation, so we find French law entering the Iraq *wilayahs* in the late 19th Century via the Ottomans.[28]

---

24   Ahmed Zaki Al-Khayyat, *A History of Lawyers in Iraq*, 52.

25   Abdul Rahmaan Kedur, "Judicial Development," 37.

26   Ahmed Zaki Al-Khayyat, *A History of Lawyers*, 55.

27   Abdul Rahmaan Kedur, "Judicial Development, 37.

28   Abdul Hameed Kuba, *Judicial Organizations*, 115.

In line with trends noted by the Ottoman leadership, laws were increasingly codified in the 19th and early 20th centuries. A commission established by the Ottomans produced the *Mecelle*, a sixteen volume work completed between 1869 and 1876. Since the foundation of the laws being reviewed and codified were primarily based on *Sharia*, the *Mecelle* was the first effort to codify elements of Islamic laws by harmonizing interpretations and clarifying elements.[29] Family law issues remained with the religious authorities, however the *Mecelle* covered the gamut of civil law starting with the "Book on Sales" and ending with the "Book on the Judiciary". The *Mecelle* is arranged in books and parts according to commonly known subjects in ordinary jurisprudence. The judgments are given in 1851 articles arranged serially and in a similar manner to that used in modern laws so that they can be easily referred to and accessed.

The last update to the *Mecelle* was published in in the eighth month of the Islamic calendar, or *Sha'aban*, 1293 A.H. / 1882 A.D. The codification is a milestone in that it marks the first point at which the personal status of followers of all religions and faiths could be adjudicated by the courts using the same laws and guidance regardless of the faith of the claimants. The *Mecelle* is therefore the first collection of Islamic jurisprudence, de facto laws, and regulations in the civil domain.

I would like to reiterate that the movement towards codification of the civil law in Iraq, in the present sense of creating a universal understanding of the law that is applied equally to any and all claimants, started in the late Ottomans era with the publication of the *Mecelle*. Although influenced by processes and systems in Europe at the time, the *Mecelle* is nonetheless a product of the centuries of Islamic jurisprudence and thought that grew from the application of *Sharia* law.

---

29 "Mecelle," Oxford Islamic Studies Online, accessed 26 July 2011, http://www.oxfordislamicstudies.com/article/opr/t125/e1492.

The *Mecelle* became a general civil law throughout the Ottoman Empire. It included provisions on civil and commercial matters still central to business today, such as sales, leases, special recorded obligations similar to the common law concept of recognizance, money transfers, mortgages, damage awards, law of companies, and so on. These provisions were of course derived largely from the jurisprudence in the Hanafi branch of Islam since this was the official faith of the Ottoman state. Other faiths were not taken into consideration because the Collection was issued on the Sultan's order. Where the *Mecelle* was silent on an issue, judges could resort to Islamic jurisprudence.[30] The *Mecelle* remained in force in former Ottoman territories until well into the 20th century when countries, newly independent or under new authority, issued updated codes.[31]

Ottoman leadership developed the *Mecelle* and other reforms as part of a campaign to modernize the state in order to improve competitiveness with European countries in the field of communications, trade, and industrial relations. Europe's rapid and far-reaching progress in trade and technical areas strongly influenced top Ottoman officials. The officials reacted pragmatically by searching the foreign systems for ideas that would strengthen the Ottoman state. For example, the officials adopted the idea of generating a real property record within the government for connecting real estate transactions, which modernized real estate transactions throughout the empire in the span of a few decades.

The exposure to the systems stoking growth in Europe also highlighted another reason for the issuance of the *Mecelle* from a political and administrative point of view: efficiency. Islamic jurisprudence had grown very sophisticated, but by its nature it did not offer clear guidance to citizens trying to live and prosper in the

---

[30]   Abdul Rahmaan Kedur, "Judicial Development," 37.

[31]   "Mecelle," Wikipedia, last modified 19 November 2013, http://en.wikipedia.org/wiki/Mecelle.

territories. The provisions of Islamic jurisprudence were distributed in books from Islamic scholars in the form of *fiqh* that illustrated certain principles as applied to a variety of contexts. Since the scholars were not within a hierarchical structure, each case may have any number of contrary opinions that could be applied by judges depending on their interpretation of provisions. Consequently, judges grew overwhelmed with the *fatwas* (edicts), interpretations and statements issued by religious experts from a range of perspectives, and justice itself became a slow and unreliable process.[32] Previously, the Ottoman state had passed a number of laws. For example, Sultan Suleiman the Magnificent directed the drafting of a *Law Nama* that included clauses on discretionary penalties, land rights, definitions of state land and revenues, and military and administrative matters. It also directed that a register of sentences passed by personal status courts be kept.

---

[32] Abdul Rahmaan Ibrahim al-Humaythi, *The Judiciary and Its System in the Quran and Sunna*, 1st ed. (Mecca: Um al-Kura University Press, 1409 AH), p 296.

CHAPTER TWO

The Judiciary & Courts During the British Occupation

Britain captured Basrah in late 1914 as an early part of its campaign against the Ottoman Empire in WWI.[33] Instead of keeping the laws and judicial institutions of the Ottoman era intact, as required by international norms at that time, the British military administration allowed, or failed to prevent while their attention was diverted to military concerns, the existing court structure to collapse when the Turkish administrators fled. Ad hoc military and civilian orders were used until the British issued a more substantial body of law called the Iraqi Occupied Territories Code (Iraqi Code), derived from the laws Britain established previously in India and some Turkish law. The Iraqi Code was eventually applied throughout the areas of Iraq controlled by Britain, starting with Basrah, Al-Emaraa and Nassiriya. These laws were only applied in larger towns. In villages, the British military administration applied Tribal Criminal and Civil Disputes Regulations drawn up by the British Governor Henry Dewes based in large part on Indian Border Crimes Regulation. As most of the trained judges left with the Turks and remaining court staff had been trained on laws and systems in Turkish, the new British efforts in Arabic and English were primarily administered by British military and, eventually, civilian political officers.

---

[33] John Keegan, *An Illustrated History of the First World War* (New York: Alfred A. Knopf, 2001), 203.

The British established courts under the Iraqi Code in Basrah in April 1915, approximately five months after the initial occupation. These courts started to use Arabic in their proceedings instead of the Turkish language. Colonel Percy Fox, who would later become Sir Percy Fox and Civil Administrator of Mesopotamia, was appointed the first civil officer in Basra.

On March, 11, 1917, Britain occupied Baghdad and the Turkish judges left the city. The courts were either completely or nearly suspended throughout the city. The Turkish officials left, too, destroying the records. In Baghdad, only two courts held hearings, one *Shari'a* Court and one *Sulih,* or Magistrate, Court located in the government palace adjacent to the Governor's palace. British policy remained unsettled. As WWI raged, military law was applied by the British in Baghdad until the end of 1917 as a temporary measure to fill gaps in civilian administrative structures left by the departure of the Turks.[34]

British policy began to settle through the influence of senior civilian and military personnel such as Gertrude Bell and Colonel Percy Fox, who reportedly became a knight along the way. By 1918, the British had gained control over most of Iraq, but the Ottoman systems had been actively or inadvertently dismantled since the capture of Basrah nearly four years earlier. In the midst of on-going internal policy debates over how to engage with the different ethnic and social groups in Iraq, British administrators decided to set up more permanent civil offices and institutions. Thus the British forces formed the British Civil Administration in Iraq headed by Sir Percy Cox to develop civilian systems to supplant the temporary systems emplaced by the still much larger British military mission. In order to organize the courts, the Civil Administration sought the assistance of Sir Edgar Bonham Carter who previously established the British Empire's legal system in Sudan.

---

[34] Abdul Hameed Kuba, *Judicial Organizations*, 91.

While awaiting the completion of Sir Bonham Carter's report, the British re-established a Magistrate Court and a *Shari'a* Court in Baghdad in July 1917. The remainder of the former Ottomon territories remained without formal courts, however British political officers were granted some authority for handling disputes pending the completion of the review. Beginning in mid-1917, Bonham Carter assessed the status of courts, including available resources and staff, and legal frameworks at that time and made suggestions so that they might resume functioning as quickly as possible. In the report, which was well received by the British Administrators, Bonham Carter recommended restoring the Personal Status Courts for Sunni Moslems to the position they had during the Ottoman era due to the high respect Iraqis accorded them.[35] The report also recognized the utility of the general court structure under the Ottomans and, with some practical modifications to reflect available staffing and changes in civil authority, called for the restoration of courts with limited jurisdiction and an appellate structure.[36]

In December, 1917 the British Civil Administration adopted Bonham Carter's initial recommendations. The revised court structure was largely familiar and maintained in large part Ottoman rules of procedure. It was defined by several characteristics that marked important moves in the modernization of the Iraqi court system: 1) Arabic replaced Turkish as the language of court actions and documents, 2) the further development of professional classes of court actors in Iraq, including judges, administrators, and lawyers were encouraged by the new structure through the consolidation of courts, increased pay scales, and by internalizing the court systems

---

[35] Gertrude Bell, *Review of the Civil Administration of Mesopotamia* (London: H.M. Stationery Office, 1920), 92. Accessed through http://www.archive.org/stream/reviewofciviladmin00iraqrih_djvu.txt, 30 July 2011.

[36] Bell, *Review of the Civil Administration,* citing Sir Edgar Bonham Carter, at 93.

within Iraq.[37] The courts established at the end of 1917 went through some additional fine tuning but by 1919 the British established the following court structure in the former Ottomon territories:

1- Court of Appeal: established in Baghdad and was regarded as a high court for the whole of Mesopotamia. This became a final court of appeal as the linkage to the Ottoman Court of Revision was severed and the British did not establish a Cassation Court in Iraq at the time. The court of appeal consisted of a British chief justice and two Iraqi judges, or *hokkam*. Importantly, the change combined all appellate actions within Iraq into a single location at Baghdad as opposed to the lower appellate courts in some *wilayats* and an option for further appeal to Istanbul under the Turks.

2- *Bada'a* [Courts of First Instance]: courts established in Baghdad, Hilla, Baquba, Basrah, and Mosul with British judges presiding as Presidents and Iraqi judges supporting. These courts addressed civil and commercial cases, including personal status issues for non-Muslims in both established and mobile courts.[38]

3- *Al-Sulih* (called "Peace" or "Small Causes" Courts by the British) Courts,[39] which were established in Baghdad, Basra, Mosul, Umarah, and Kirkuk by 1919. The initial court in

---

37 Bell, *Review of the Civil Administration,* citing Sir Edgar Bonham Carter, at 101-102.

38 Bell, *Review of the Civil Administration,* at 95. The original structure, set-up in December 1917, only established *Shari'a* Courts for Sunni Muslims, with the courts "authorized to refer this type of case [personal status] respectively to a Shi'ah religious priest or to the Christian or Jewish religious authorities." *Id.*

39 *Id.* at 91. These small claims courts were re-established in Baghdad in July 1917 but not extended to other parts of the country until the December 1917 declaration that followed Bonham Carter's report.

Baghdad was presided over by a former deputy of the *Shari'a* court in Baghdad. The courts had the same jurisdiction as defined under the Ottoman system, however after July 1917 court business was conducted in Arabic. In smaller jurisdictions, judges of the Court of First Instance, *Shari'a* Court judges, Political Officers and others could be called on to officiate as Peace Judges with varying powers.[40]

4- *Shari'a* (Islamic) Courts: established in line with the system under the Ottomans following the large reform in the 19th century to address cases related to the personal status issues of Muslims. Starting from the single court re-established in 1917 to manage cases from Sunni Muslims, the *Shari'a* courts grew to number thirty courts handling either Sunni or Shia cases, in separate courts, by 1920.[41] The decisions of these courts were ratified by the Islamic *Shari'a* Cassation Board established in August, 1918.[42]

5- Criminal Courts: the British created a hierarchy of criminal courts of four classes separate from actions for civil or commercial causes. These included a Court of Session and First, Second, and Third Class Magistrates Courts. Three magistrates presided over a Court of Session, and more important districts would have a British judge stationed. A Court of Session decision required confirmation from the Civil Commissioner. The verdicts of High Criminal Court were subject to the approval of the Civil Commissioner who was regarded as the final judicial authority at the time.[43]

---

[40]   Bell, *Review of the Civil Administration,* at 98.

[41]   *Id.* at 91.

[42]   *Id.*

[43]   Ahmed Zaki Al-Khayyat, *A History of Lawyers,* at 54.

From the time of occupation in 1914 onwards, court proceedings were conducted in Arabic. The three distinct judicial systems in the Turkish *wilayats* of Baghdad, Mosul and Basra were unified as part of a national system. By 1919 the British had also initiated another reform that reverberated through the next century of judicial development. Under the guidance of Sir Edgar Bonham Carter, the administration of justice was brought into the administrative unit of the British in a form intended to be similar to the Justice Ministries Bonham Carter had reviewed in continental Europe.[44] Bonham Carter became the first administrative head of justice administration as Judicial Secretary, which meant that he could not perform judicial functions.

The British administration replaced the Ottoman Penal Code with the Baghdad Penal Code nationally on November 21, 1918. It was so called because it was first applied in Baghdad and then extended to the rest of Iraq. Similarly, the Baghdad Criminal Procedure Code was promulgated and entered into force in December 1919. Through the provisions of these two codes, the courts throughout Iraq were harmonized under the same systems, rules and laws.

Managing the business of the judicial system in Iraq faced great difficulties when the Turks left, in part because few Iraqis had studied law. The British responded with several enduring contributions, including re-opening Baghdad Law School in 1919. By the time of the Treaty of Versailles in 1919, Britain occupied most of Iraq under a complicated Mandate that left many pre-war promises unfulfilled and opened deep chasms within the British government on how the Mandate in Iraq should be fulfilled in the post-war environment.[45] Although many British administrative elements, including justice sector development, solidified between 1914 and 1920, some groups within Iraq became disaffected and uprisings erupted throughout Iraq in 1920.

---

[44] Bell, *Review of the Civil Administration,* at 97.

[45] Charles Tripp, *A History of Iraq* (Cambridge: Cambridge University Press, 2000), 39.

CHAPTER THREE

The Judiciary & Courts Under the British Mandate, Monarchy, and Republic Periods

By judicial system we mean the general Judicial Authority along with the courts and administrative institutions necessary for functioning. As such, the judicial system includes the organizational question of how judges are set up by rank, types of judges, systems for appointment, considerations for promotion, retirement, and dismissal, and even frameworks for accountability. Both the Ottomans and the British created bodies of laws and policies related to many of these elements, however once Iraq started along the road to independence it gained a domestic source of ultimate authority: a constitution. This work is an overview of how the role of judges and courts evolved over a very long period of time. The political and economic environment shaping that evolution was rarely more dynamic than during the transition period from Ottoman rule, through British mandate and then into the monarch and republic phases of Iraq's history.

Many other books review the events, personalities and politics during that period. My goal with this chapter is to offer a snapshot of the administrative changes made to the judiciary and the courts. From our current vantage point in time we can see that the elements of judicial independence hinted at during Ottoman rule and nurtured in some ways by the growth of Islam, combined with the increasing sophistication of the courts within a constitutional system, greatly increased the pressure on actors to abide by modern principles of justice. We can also draw comfort in the fact that Iraq can, if it so chooses, draw on nearly 100 years of experience with different "modern" systems and structures that sought to balance judicial, executive and legislative powers in order to bring access to justice to communities regardless of sectarian, ethnic or economic backgrounds.

I offer a brief word on the political context within which the judicial system evolved between 1914-1958. As discussed above, the British occupied Basrah by the end of 1914 against the backdrop of WWI. By 1917, the British had taken control over all of Iraq, or Mesopotamia as it was called at the time, and more earnestly approached the need for concrete national administrative systems. After WWI ended in 1918, negotiations between many parties resulted in a Class A Mandate for British control over Iraq in 1920. The result disappointed many and created a very tense political landscape locally while the western world struggled to rebuild after WWI. The League of Nation Mandate created a number of obligations for the British, however many factions in both the British administration and the greater Iraq territories disagreed over how those obligations would best be addressed. Some factions in Iraq expected independence after WWI ended. After several years of confusion, the British instead organized a referendum in 1921 to create a monarchy that would remain closely linked with the British until Iraq joined the League of Nations in 1932. The British began developing the superficial structures of democracy in the form of elected advisory councils and assemblies early in their control of Iraq. People were suspect of the hand-picked assemblies, which in any event lacked more than advisory powers in most important areas. There were several coups between 1932 and 1958 generated by military, ethnic and religious faction; all told there were fifty eight governments in the years spanning 1922 to 1958.[46] Investments in the judiciary and court structure continued, however, as most understood the lessons from history that trust in government is greatly increased when people have faith in the independence of the judiciary and the ability of the courts to fairly resolve disputes.

In 1958, Iraq departed the period of the monarchy and became a republic. Between 1921 and a major overhaul of the judicial and court structures in 1977, which is considered in the next chapter, Iraq led the Middle East in developing modern legal codes and systems. However, challenges to the independence of the judiciary also arose. As the final barrier to dictatorial tendencies, the judiciary bore a heavy weight during periods of political turmoil. The period included the creation of national structures for both judges and courts, the exploration of administrative systems that balanced the need for judicial independence with political demands, and several approaches to addressing the needs of different religious and ethnic groups within Iraq through the justice system.

After the monarchy was established in 1921, the judicial system continued as it was under the British occupation. As discussed, the system maintained much of the Ottoman system but also created domestic structures that carried forward into the new system. The Constitution of the Kingdom of Iraq, enacted in 1925, affirmed many of the structures then in place and, in Article 71, the independence of the judiciary. Regulations and conditions governing the appointment of both civil and religious judges continued as they were under the British occupation until Iraq passed the Law of Judges and *Qodat* Act, No. 31 of 1929, at *Tha Al-Kidda,* 1347 A.H. (1929 Act) as required by the Constitution. As the country continued to grow, the government enacted additional revisions and new acts related to administrative systems (including the role of judicial

---

[46]   Christopher Catherwood, *Churchill's Folly: How Winston Churchill Created Modern Iraq* (New York: Carroll & Graf Publishers, 2004), 217.

committees or councils), ranks and organization of the judiciary, types of courts and jurisdiction, and accountability mechanisms. In general, the changes created an increasingly complex system that returned to earlier efforts to support judicial independence. Over time new institutions, such as the Office of Judicial Supervision and the role of Prosecutors, were created to ensure accountability within the courts.

This was the first Iraqi law regulating the judicial system, and is considered a milestone because it contributed to the growing status and independence of the judiciary. Building on historic developments, the law confirms separate classes for judges, civil (*Hokkam*) and religious (*Qodat*),[47] and details administrative elements such as conditions for probation, transfer and accountability. The law further defined the requirements for the appointment of a Qadi and a judge, which was a major step forward from the initial period of British occupation when political officers and Iraqi staff were assigned to different posts without clear standards. Many British judges remained in the court system at the time of independence, however they were not subject to the requirements of this law.

According to Article 9, a candidate for judge needed, at a minimum, to be an Iraqi citizen, to have an L.L.B, to have at least two years of experience in the courts or in a legal position with a Ministry, to be at least twenty-five years old, to speak Arabic well, and to have a "good reputation". The Act notes that a religious judge should have the same requirements as a civil judge. Article 10 also allows for individuals to be posted from the body of jurists that do not meet the minimum requirements if there are not enough qualified candidates.[48]

---

47   Judges and *Qodat* Act, No. 31 of 1929, Article (2) defines a judge as one that presides over a civil court (including criminal, commercial and private actions), and a *Qadi* as one that presides over a *Shari'a* court. Readers will note that this book uses "civil court" to include all non-religious courts.

48   Judges and *Qodat* Act, No. 31 of 1929, Article (10).

The 1929 Act established the first judicial committee in Iraqi history, the *Hokkam* and *Qodat* Affairs Committee (1929 Committee), to look after the affairs of both civil (*hokkam*) and religious (*qodat*) judges.[49] The 1929 Committee consisted of a chair, who was usually the Chief Justice of the Cassation Court established by the Act, and two additional members, one of which was an official from the Ministry of Justice or a magistrate appointed by the Minster, and the second a judge that could be brought in depending on the nature of the matter under discussion. For example, the third member could be a judge from the Cassation Court if the 1929 Committee was discussing the promotion of civil judges or it could be either a Sunni or Shia representative from the Council of Religious Affairs to accommodate special considerations for the affairs of religious judges.[50]

The 1929 Act entrusted the Committee with a number of responsibilities related to the nomination and development of civil and religious judges:

- The 1929 Committee nominated candidates to be judges and Qadis through the Minister of Justice for royal approval. Note that the nominating authority was absolute, so the Minister of Justice could not forward names unless they were generated by the Committee.

- The 1929 Committee was also responsible for recommending judges for promotion, however promotions required the approval of the Minister of Justice. If the Minister rejected nominees, the Committee could then still

---

[49] Judges and *Qodat* Act, No. 31 of 1929.

[50] Judges and *Qodat* Act, No. 31 of 1929, Article (3-1).

put forward a short list of three names for the Minister to select from. [51]

- The 1929 Committee recommended judges for transfer. As opposed to nominations, however, the Minister could refuse the Committee's recommendation with justification or transfer judges without the recommendation of the Committee.[52]

Reflecting the importance of the judicial system in the multi-ethnic and economically diverse country, the 1929 Act established several provisions related to judicial accountability. First, the 1929 Committee was empowered to review a judge's performance at the request of the Minister. After review, the 1929 Committee could was also empowered to reprimand, demote, or dismiss a judge found to be at fault [53] or refer a lower judge to a criminal court on approval of the Minister. In a case relating to a judge in the Court of Cassation the matter would be referred to the Council of Ministers rather than to the Minister of Justice alone.[54] The Act proscribed mechanisms for managing trials of judges if the Minister or Council of Ministers, as the case may be, deemed a trial necessary after reviewing the 1929 Committee's recommendation. Different provisions were triggered based on whether the trial was related to the judge's official duties and on the judge's position.[55]

---

[51]   Judges and *Qodat* Act, No. 31 of 1929, Article (12-2). Article (12-2) of the Law of Judges and Qadis states that when there is a vacancy in higher judicial jobs, the promotion to this job is made by order of the Minister on the recommendation of the Committee.

[52]   Judges and *Qodat* Act, No. 31 of 1929, Article (13).

[53]   Judges and *Qodat* Act, No. 31 of 1929, Article (18) and Article (22).

[54]   Judges and *Qodat* Act, No. 31 of 1929, Article (25).

[55]   Judges and *Qodat* Act, No. 31 of 1929, Article (27).

In 1943 Iraq revised the law related to the judicial system. Law No. 68 of 1943 (1943 Act) revised earlier provisions, including those related to the functions of the 1929 Committee, and created the Committee for Judges and *Qodat* (1943 Committee). The updated 1943 Committee was still chaired by the Chief Justice. The other two positions were both selected by the Minister of Justice, one from the Ministry and one selected from the judges of the Court of Cassation or, if the issue related to a *Shari'a* Court issue, from one of the two *Shari'a* Cassation Boards. The 1943 Committee retained responsibilities regarding nomination, promotion and maintaining accountability.

The 1943 Act further refined the professional parameters of the judiciary by establishing additional classifications within both civil and religious judicial ranks and by creating a new junior post of Deputy Judge.[56] An individual that met basic requirements could be assigned as a Deputy Judge for a two year probationary period. The shortage of candidates with the academic and professional credentials to be judges still weighed heavily on the government's considerations, however, as the 1943 Act also allowed Deputy Judges to be used in more senior roles if needed. In the same vein, the 1943 Act also allowed a religious judge to be appointed as a Deputy Judge if there is no civil court available in an area. While professional standards continued to grow, we see that the administration of justice retained a fundamental pragmatism.

The 1943 Act generated classes of judges and courts that reflected the modernization of Iraq as oil and urban elements became increasingly important. The 1943 Act refined the classes of judges within both the civil and religious ranks that related to length of service and competence. Civil judges began at the lowest rank of five and ascended to one, and religious judges were divided into four ranks. In relevant part, the 1943 Act outlined the following:

---

[56]   Judges and *Qodat* Act, No. 68 of 1943, Article (4).

A. The ranks of civil judges are five. The first is the highest and the fifth is the lowest and as follows:

1- The Chief Justice of the Court of Appeal, his Deputy, judges sitting on the Court, and Chief Justices of Courts of First Instanceare first rank;

2- Deputies of Chief Justices of Courts of First Instance, judges assigned to manage courts alone, judges sitting in Real Estate Courts, and the First Judge in *Sulih* and Criminal Courts in Baghdad, Basra, and Mosul are second and third ranks;

3- Lower judges judges sitting in *Sulih* courts, Courts of First Instance, Criminal Courts , and Heads of Implementation Departments are fourth and fifth ranks.

B. The *Qadis* are four ranks as follows:

1- The two chairmen of the Councils for Religious Affairs are first rank;

2- Members of Councils for Religious Affairs and *Qadis* in Baghdad, Basra, and Mosel are first and second ranks;

3- The *Qadis* in centers of governorates are second and third rank;

4- The *Qadis* in Kadaa and Nahiyya are fourth ranks;

Turning to the courts themselves, the successive governments applied a similarly pragmatic approach during this period to expanding both the reach and reliability of courts. The British judicial system operated court systems that retained much of the structure established in 1917. However, the 1925 Constitution of Iraq created a new

Court of Cassation.[57] Headquartered in Baghdad, the Court of Cassation had both original and appellate jurisdiction until changes in the law in 1945, discussed below, when it was restrained only to its Cassation functions.[58]

The demands on the judges and staff of the new Iraqi judicial system are illustrated by the number and types of cases. Between early 1924 and June of 1925, the judicial system addressed the following:[59]

Type of Case	Number of Cases Heard
Courts of First Instance	931
Sulih Courts	51118
Personal Status Cases of Non-Muslims	1337
Serious Criminal Cases	629
Appellate Criminal Cases (date of original action unknown)	1323
Lawsuits without Summary Judgment	5719
Lawsuits with Summary Judgment	76339
Sunni *Shari'a* Actions	779
Shiite *Shari'a* Actions	6773
Court of Cassation Cases	963
Appealed Cases Through 1924	304
Total	153233

---

57   1925 Constitution of Iraq, Article (81).

58   Law No. 3 of 1945.

59   *The Lawyer*, 1925 Edition. [Editor's Note: limited information available on this publication].

The number of courts in Iraq in 1924:

Type of Court	Number of Active Courts
Court of Appeal	1
Courts of First Instance	5
Single Judge Courts	7
Sulih Courts	9
Shari'a Cassation Boards	2
Courts of Personal Status	27

We have discussed the evolution of the legislative framework governing judges in this period through the impact of the original law in 1929 and subsequent revisions in 1932, 1943, and 1945. The courts themselves, however, remained structured largely as outlined in the Declaration based on Bonham Carter's report in 1917 until the government issued the Law of the Formation of Courts, No. 3 of 1945. (Courts Law 1945).

The Courts Law 1945 established new detailed procedures for the Court of Cassation. It also divided Iraq into the six judicial districts of Baghdad, Basra, Mosul, Hillah, Diyala, and Kirkuk; these districts are the foundation of the modern administrative units of the court system in Iraq. The Chief Justice of the high court in each of the six jurisdictions was in charge of the administration of all courts in that district and responsible for organizing work within it under the direction of the relevant Court of Appeal.[60]

Each of the six district administrative offices came under the direction of one of the three Courts of Appeal. Thus Baghdad Appellate Court had authority over the lower courts of the Baghdad, Hillah and Diyala court districts, Mosul Appellate Court covered the districts of

---

[60] Courts Formation Law, No. 3 of 1945, Article (6).

Mosul and Kirkuk, while the Basra Court of Appeal dealt with the single district of Basrah.

The Courts Law 1945 divided the Courts of First Instance into two types: Courts of First Instance with Limited Jurisdiction, which were limited to cases not exceeding ID 500,[61] cases based on a fixed fee, or cases without a defined value, and Courts of First Instance with Unlimited Jurisdiction, which was logically not limited by financial amounts it the type of case that it could hear.[62] The Courts Law of 1943 continued the trend of increasing the number of locally accessible courts by establishing a *Sulih* court and a Court of Personal Status wherever a Court of First Instance was established. It also stipulated that lawsuits be suspended (except for urgent cases) from 15th July to the end of September every year. This suspension of hearings was called the annual court holidays and accommodated both the heat of summer and the typical dates of the major Islamic holiday period of Ramadan.[63]

---

[61]   Editor's Note: Anecdotal records indicate that 1 Iraqi Dinar was worth USD 4 in 1943. The 1943 jurisdictional limit of approximately USD 2000 for the Limited Jurisdiction Courts would be roughly equivalent to USD 25,000 in modern purchasing power. http://www.measuringworth.com/ppowerus/result.php, accessed 15 August 2011. Unfortunately, the amounts of jurisdiction were locked into legislation and were not allowed to adjust to inflation or other considerations automatically so the court's jurisdiction eventually became too low in many people's opinion. As a result, in later years higher courts were forced by the rigid jurisdiction requirements in the static law to address cases that would have originally been routed to the lower courts. This illustrates a recurring problem with British and post-British legislation in Iraq, which tended to create rigid limits for both jurisdiction and financial penalties in legislation rather than allowing inflationary, or at least regulatory, adjustments.

[62]   Courts Formation Law, No. 3 of 1945, Article (9).

[63]   Courts Formation Law, No. 3 of 1945, Article (15).

In 1945 the government again reviewed the organization of the judiciary, enacting the Judicial Service Law, No. 27 of 1945. (Judicial Law 1945). Among the most important provisions of the new law was the re-establishment of Judges and *Qodat* Committee with a new structure: It was still chaired by the Chief Justice of the Court of Cassation but now included two justices from the Court of Cassation and two officials from the Ministry of Justice appointed by the Minister. The law included the President of the Sunni Council for Religious Affairs and President of the Shiite Council for Religious Affairs as members of the Committee in place of the members from the Cassation Court when the Committee looked into a matter relating to *Qadis*.[64]

The Judicial Law 1945 created the position of Judicial Inspectors, a critical step towards extending accountability throughout the court system. Judicial Inspectors were charged with oversight over the work of judges operating below the Court of Cassation, *Qadis* sitting in personal status courts, the work of councils addressing personal status issues for other religions, and over officials granted forms of Judicial Authority. Since Judicial Inspectors worked for the Ministry, the Judicial Law 1945 left supervision of the Court of Cassation with the office of the Chief Justice in order to maintain independence at the highest levels of the court.[65] Similarly, the Judicial Law 1945 protected judges and *qadi* from

---

[64] Judicial Service Law, No. 27 of 1945, Article (4-2). The Presidents of *Sharia* Cassation Councils are considered members in the committee, replacing the two justices from the Cassation Court, when the case concerns a Qadi. If a President of the Sharia Cassation Council is absent, he will be replaced by the eldest member.

[65] Judicial Service Law, No. 27 of 1945, Article (1-23). According to this law, the Minister is entitled to supervise and check on all judges, Qadis, civil courts, personal status courts, non-Muslim councils, and officials authorized with judicial authority. He can also appoint judicial inspectors or mandate a judge or an official for this purpose. However, inspection of work of Court of Cassation is carried out only by its Chief Justice. *Id.*

detention or arrest without the prior approval of the Minister of Justice unless directly witnessed committing a crime.[66] In effect, this provision assisted in ensuring that local authorities could not unduly influence the judges living within their communities through the use of, or threatened use of, detention or arrest by requiring the police to coordinate any action against judges with the national Minister.

The Judicial Law 1945 increased the requirements and benefits of judges, further raising the bar of the profession. New candidates now needed three years of experience instead of two.[67] The new Law granted judges and *Qadis* special benefits not exceeding 25% of their basic salaries.[68] Their base salaries were further increased over those established nearly twenty years earlier under Law No (31) of 1926 and its amendments.[69]

The Judicial Law 1945 remained in place for eleven years before the government revisited judicial systems in the Judicial Service Law, No. 58 of 1956. (Judicial Service Law 1956). The most important developments in the 1956 law were further reforms to the oversight committee that had been evolving through the decades. Renamed the Judges and *Qadis* Affairs Committee, the new law retained the Chief Justice as the Chair, but expanded membership of the committee to include the Chairman of the Judicial Investigation Commission, the Deputy Chief Justice of the Court of Cassation Court, and one official from the Ministry of Justice, who would be appointed

---

[66]   Judicial Service Law, No. 27 of 1945, Article (1-37), stating that a judge or Qadi shall not be detained or subjected to legal measures unless the Minister agrees, except for the case a crime where there are eye witnesses, in which case the Minister is merely informed.

[67]   Judicial Service Law, No. 27 of 1945, Article (5-2).

[68]   Judicial Service Law, No. 27 of 1945, Article (47), establishing that Judges and Qadis may be granted special benefits in cases the cabinet agrees on provided they should not exceed 25% of their salaries.

[69]   Judicial Service Law, No. 27 of 1945, Article (39).

annually by the Minster. As with previous committee structures, the law called for the addition of the two Presidents of Sunni and Shiite Councils for Religious Affairs when a matter involved a *qadi* from one of the two branches. [70]

One again raising the professional standards, and reflecting the increasing pool of qualified candidates, the Judicial Service Law 1956 raised the minimum age of an applicant to thirty from twenty five while also establishing experience requirements. The Law required eight years of experience in one of the judicial posts specified in Article (Five) after obtaining a degree from the College of Law, five years of experience if the candidate held a post-graduate diploma in law, or two years of experience if the candidate held a PhD in law or *Shari'a*.[71]

The Judicial Service Law 1956 also introduced several new provisions to support efforts to increase the accountability of judicial officers. For the first time, an oath of office was mandated for judges to swear before the General Assembly of the Court of Cassation. [72] In Article (49) the 1956 Law also established a council to make a comprehensive review of the position of all judges and *Qadis*. Named the Higher Judicial Council, the provisional body was tasked with

---

[70]   Judicial Service Law No. 58 of 1956, Article (5-12).

[71]   Judicial Service Law No. 58 of 1956, Article (5).

[72]   Article (8-10) of the Judicial Service Law No (58) of 195:
1-Every judge, Qadi, deputy judge, or deputy Qadi shall swear the following oath of office before they actually exercise the powers of the office: I swear by God to adjudicate justly and apply the law with honesty.
2-This oath is sworn before the full session of the Court of Cassation

deciding which judicial officers would be retained and which would be released with three months' notice.[73]

The 1956 Law continued the practice of including salary and benefit provisions within legislation. The Law raised the salary and benefits of the Chief Justice of the Court of Cassation to those of a minister, and those of the Deputy Chief Justice of the Court of Cassation to 220 Iraqi Dinar permonth. [74] Other protections and provisions consolidated management of the judiciary under the Chief Justice and continued to reflect a growing pool of qualified judges. For example, the law stipulates that no judge be transferred to a civil position without the Chief Justice's written approval,[75] and required judges and *Qadis* to retire when they attained the age of sixty three.[76]

It was again eleven years before the government revisited the laws related to the judiciary in the Law of Judicial Authority, No. 26 of 1963.

In this section we have seen the flowering of judicial independence and professionalism through the decades following the departure of the Ottomans. At the same time, it became apparent that there was a tension between the need for independence and the seeds of executive control that the British had planted, or at least fertilized, in the judicial system established after the Ottoman period in Iraq.

---

[73] Judicial Service Law No. 58 of 1956, Article (49), stating that "A Higher Judicial Council shall consist of chairman and members of the committee, two Chief Justices from Appellate Courts selected by the Minister to look into the conduct and competence of judges of second rank and below and the competence of Qadis except those of the Presidents of Sharia Cassation. Whoever proves competent the Council will assign to the rank he deserves according to this law. The Council will terminate the services of anyone who is unfit for judicial service."

[74] Judicial Service Law No. 58 of 1956, Article (1-12).

[75] Judicial Service Law No. 58 of 1956, Article (4).

[76] Judicial Service Law No. 58 of 1956, Article (53).

In its Justification section, the 1963 Law of Judicial Authority addresses this tension by noting that previous laws "were enacted under conditions in which the legislator did not consider judicial inviolability and independence of the judiciary as much as the interest of those in power." The Justification further explains that the 1963 law was specifically drafted with the intent of equalizing the Judicial and Executive powers, and heralded the arrival of the judiciary as an independent power alongside the executive and legislative powers.[77] Although keeping the same functions for the Judges and *Qadis* Affairs Committee, the 1963 Law changed the name to the Judicial Council.[78]

More dramatically, the new law also realigned the jurisdiction of the courts. You'll remember that previous governments had addressed the organization of the judiciary and the functioning of the courts separately. The Judicial Authority Law of 1963 abolished the judicial districts that were formed by the Courts Formation Law of

---

[77]   Justification, Judicial Authority Law, No. 26 of 1963.

[78]   Judicial Authority Law, No. 26 of 1963, Article (28), stating:
A) Judicial Council shall be formed chaired by Chief Justice of Court of Cassation and membership of two longest serving deputy Chief Justices of Court of Cassation and if they are not available, two longest serving justices of the Court of Cassation, Chairman of Judicial Oversight Commission and DG of Justice Office, a justice from the Court of Cassation and Chairman of Law Drafting Commission. They were appointed by the Minister and looked into issues specified by the law.
B) If chairman is absent; the longest serving deputy will take over. If the latter is absent, the longest serving justice of the Court of Cassation will take the chair.
C) The Minister has the right to appoint substitute members chosen from top officials of the Ministry and justices from the Court of Cassation to replace the absent members.
D) A member of Judicial Council can be removed for the same reason a judge is removed. The request is submitted to Chief Justice of the Council. The Council meets without the attendance of the member whose removal is requested but a substitute member attends instead. The Council's decision is final.

1945 and replaced them with more clearly defined appellate areas. In another critical move towards a harmonized justice system, the 1963 law abolished the two sectarian Councils for Religious Affairs and established a single Commission within the Court of Cassation. The former Presidents of the Religious Affairs Councils became members of the new Personal Status Commission within the Court of Cassation, and the *Qadis* within the Councils joined the Courts of Personal Status. It was a healthy initiative to once again amalgamate the Sunni and Shiite personal status laws in Iraq into one personal status law, reminiscent of the efforts of the Ottomans prior to the arrival of the British.[79]

By 1977, however, the political environment had again shifted and the Law of the Ministry of Justice, No. 101 of 1977, established the Justice Council under the Executive to manage judicial affairs in the place of the Judicial Council.[80] Under Law No. 101 of 1977, the

---

[79] Judicial Authority Law, No. 26 of 1963, Article (72).

[80] Organic Law of the Ministry of Justice, Law No. 101 of 1977, Article (2-4), which stipulates the formation of the Judicial Council and its functions as follows:

Second: It looks into salary increase, transfer, and loan of judges and Qadis, checks on their conduct and competence

Director Generals at the Ministry headquarter and institutions who are not judges shall not take part in the meetings of Justice Council when it looks in matters mentioned in Clause A of this item.

Third: A committee called The Judges' and Qadis' Affairs Committee, consisting of three Council members who are judges shall be formed at the beginning of each year to look into Disciplinary action against judges and Qadis and resolve the case in terms of provisions of Chapter Eight of Law N0 (26) of 1963 and also lawsuits resulting from its provisions. The Committee resolutions are subject to legal challenge with the General Assembly of the Court of Cassation by the Minister of Justice, the judge or the Qadi ruled against within thirty days as of the day of notification. The decision in this case is irrevocable

Justice Council, chaired by the Minister of Justice, had an expanded role of providing general advice to the Minister. [81]

Other elements of the Judicial Authority Law of 1963 remained in force until the Judicial Organization Law, No. 10. Of 1979, was passed, repealing all of the provisions and regulations of the 1963 Act. The next chapter discusses the application of the new law.

---

[81]   Law of the Ministry of Justice, No. 101 of 1977, Article (1-4).

PART 2

Growth of the Unique Iraqi system

CHAPTER FOUR

Judicial Independence Under the Judicial Organization Law No. 160 of 1977

The Judicial Organization Law of 1977 brought the global debate about judicial independence to Iraq. Speaking of judicial independence as a fundamental principle and basis for the Law, Article (2) states simply that the judiciary is independent and does not come under any authority other than that of the law. Many at the time considered this acknowledgement to be a major achievement for Iraq.

Yet the people, and certainly the courts, have been working through the challenges of interpreting these broad principles into useful systems ever since. Over the years many questions have arisen in courts, on the streets, and in political offices around the world: what is meant by judicial independence as outlined in Iraqi legislation? What provisions are provided by laws and regulations to give the principle life?

For Iraq, it seems that the test lies in assessing whether the legal and regulatory framework support the judiciary's ability to enforce constitutional provisions enshrining independence. For example all modern Iraqi constitutions contain language confirming judicial independence. But, alas, harsh reality has contradicted these provisions as successive governments have not provided the will and resources necessary to sustain an independent judiciary. As a result, some Iraqis in need have not had access to independent courts that could actively advocate on their behalf neutrally, safely and effectively.

For people outside the Middle East it may be surprising to learn that the early Islamic state respected judicial independence once the Caliphs relinquished authority for adjudication to dedicated judges as discussed above. The judge was largely independent in his judgments even though the *Walee* (Governor) maintained a right to intervene under certain circumstances. The Governor themselves would appear before a judge if an individual filed a case against him.

At the international level, the principle of judicial independence was also rising to the fore as an important ingredient for protecting the emerging individual and group rights emerging following the world wars. By 1985, judicial independence was a key theme of the Seventh UN Conference on the Prevention of Crime and the Treatment of Offenders held in Milan (Milan Conference). The Milan Conference included in its final report a set of Basic Principles on the Independence of the Judiciary,[82] which were approved by the General Assembly in the same year. The preamble to the resolution includes a recognition by the General Assembly of the weight of a judge's duty—"Whereas judges are charged with the ultimate decision over life, freedoms, rights, duties and property of citizens"[83]—and the resolution goes on to mandate that all member countries include in their constitutions or laws a clause confirming the principle of judicial independence.[84]

---

[82]   Seventh United Nations Conference on the Prevention of Crime and the Treatment of Offenders. Milan, 1985. A/CONF.121/22/Rev.1 at 59.

[83]   General Assembly resolutions 40/32 of 29 November 1985 and 40/146 of 13 December 1985, http://www2.ohchr.org/english/law/indjudiciary.htm, accessed 16 April 2012.

[84]   *Id.*

This Milan view of judicial independence finds support in Article 10of the Universal Declaration of Human Rights, which states: "Everyone is entitled in full equality to a fair and public hearing by an independent and impartial tribunal, in the determination of his rights and obligations and of any criminal charge against him."[85] Since the other branches have highly visible elements of power and authority, such as weapons for the executive and money for the legislature, the ability of the judiciary to perform its role rests on constitutional and societal bulwarks defining its independence. Any breach of the bulwarks allows the money or physical authority of the other branches to erode the foundation of judicial authority. Over time, society is left without the judicial support necessary for a healthy nation.

Outside of the UN the political and social forces were more divided. Most understood that that the judiciary had its own peculiar qualities in terms of tasks, qualifications, and needs that differentiated it from other public service units. However, some regarded the judiciary as a power independent of the executive and legislative powers while others considered it simply an extension of the executive's enforcement role that required minimal procedural protections to allow impartiality.

Below I discuss these two views.

---

[85]   http://www.un.org/en/documents/udhr/index.shtml#a10, accessed 16 April 2012.

CHAPTER FIVE

One View on the Role of the Judiciary in a Modern State

The advocates of the first view maintain that a state consists of three distinct, independent powers. This is the perspective captured in the Basic Principles of Judicial Independence formulated at the Milan Conference and discussed above. These three powers in a state are generally grouped as the legislative power, which generates the laws based on constitutional authority; the Judicial Authority, which interprets and applies the laws to issues and cases; and the executive power, which enforces the laws as guided through the decisions of the judiciary. Accordingly, this view interprets judicial independence to mean that judicial authority is distinct from the executive and legislative powers just as the executive is distinct from the legislative. The independence comes from its inherent properties and the nature of the tasks fulfilled by the judges and cannot be retracted through fiat from either of the other branches. In this view, a Judicial Authority completely free from the executive and legislative powers is considered an integral part of the rule of law because it allows individual and government entities to operate within well understood rules. The interplay between the three powers is therefore able to protect individual and societal rights, hindering the rise of a totalitarian regime.

U.S. Supreme Court Chief Justice Story said that "[i]n human governments, there are only two binding powers: the power of weapon and the power of laws. If the judges who wield the power of laws are not audacious and not free from a taint of blame, the power of weapon will certainly dominate, resulting in the domination of the military over the civilian rule"[86] I add to Justice Story's comment only to say that Iraq's history has shown that even an audacious judge will struggle to perform to minimum standards of justice if constrained directly or indirectly by another authority. An independent Judicial Authority allows a citizen to bring a case against a public authority to review any legal irregularity that harms him/her. Moreover, having a free Judicial Authority should foil any attempt to set special or extraordinary tribunals.[87] A free Judicial Authority is available to safeguard citizens' rights, freedom and property from encroachment by the acts of other citizens. Without this power, the reasoning goes, society will be deprived of legal constraints against extortion and aggression from not only government, but also from other citizens and private actors like business that may have economic, religious or social power over individuals. If the judiciary is not independent, and is without viable guarantees to keep it independent of the other two powers, especially the executive power, it cannot stand against them and thus fails to fulfill its mission.[88] Surprisingly for some, this harms the other branches of government as well as individuals as inter-branch turmoil undermines markets and general stability.

Dr. Mohammed Ussfur, an active proponent of this school of thought in academic works on governance in the Middle East, summarizes the above:

• The judiciary is a power and not a public utility to be "administered".

• The judiciary is a specialized institution requiring highly developed skill sets. The use of language by judges is like

---

[86]   Dr. Mohammed Ussfur, *The Independence of the Judicial Authority*, 45.

[87]   Dr. Mohammed Ussfur, *Judicial Authority*, at 49.

[88]   *Id.* at 4.

the use of a scalpel by a surgeon. The fact that most people can use a butter knife does not mean that they should attempt surgery. Similarly, the work of a judge should not be manipulated by untrained actors.

- To be effective in line with the Milan Congress and the Universal Declaration of Human Rights, the judiciary must remain an impartial institution. It cannot operate if its decisions are effected by political winds.[89]

Dr. Ussfur and others have defined specific constitutions, legislative, and reglatory requirements for protecting judicial independence:

- The executive power cannot dismiss or transfer a judge.

- The promotion of a judge is not subject to the approval of the executive power.

- The pay and benefits of a judge are not subject to the approval of the executive power.

- Judges come under the authority of a special law defining their responsibilities, benefits, and penalties for malfeasance.[90]

---

[89]   *Id.* at 160.

[90]   Mohammed Al-Ashmawi and Abdul Wahab Al-Ashmawi, *Procedural Rules of the Egyptian Judiciary*, 32; Dr. Ramzi Saif, *Manual on the Interpretation of Civil and Commercial Trial Law*, 43. Prof. Mohammed Al-Ashmawi, Dr Abdul Wahab Al-Ashmawi, and Dr. Saif support Dr. Ussfur's call to provide these assurances as a minimum to achieve the principle of judicial independence though they do not give their opinion on the principle of separation of a state into three independent branches. Mohammed Al-Ashmawi and Abdul Wahaab Al-Ashmawi, *Procedural Rules*, at 32; Dr. Ramzi Saif, *Manual on Interpretation* at 43.

CHAPTER SIX

A Second View on the Role of the Judiciary in a Modern (Democratic) State

The advocates of this view posit that a state consists of two powers: the legislative power which enacts the laws, and the executive power which applies the laws. They regard the judiciary as an extension of the executive function rather than as an independent entity. Consequently, adherents of this view consider the judiciary one of many government bodies that have independent functions, such as the police, but which are part of a single umbrella for the purposes of generating policy and effecting administration.[91]

In addition to the historical pressures remaining from the centrally-focused Ottoman and British colonial administration, Iraq was part of the battleground between democratic and communist systems known as the cold war in other parts of the world. The former colonial systems tended to limit judicial independence out of a desire to focus central authority on executive officials that could be more easily managed than the comparative anarchy of a three-branch, fully-functioning, democratic system. This arrangement was deemed more efficient or, in other cases, necessary due to the exigencies of the geography of the Middle East and Africa. The cold war upheaval added communist perspectives that advocated for

---

[91] Dr. Thurwat Anees al-Seyoutti. "Committed Judiciary and Revolutionary Judiciary." *Al-Adala Journal*, No. 1 (2nd Year of Publication): 59.

limited judicial independence out of a belief that cases brought by the state, or allowed by the state between other parties on behalf of the proletariat, should further the ends of the social revolution, i.e. a communist state. This type of "state focused" and policy-oriented legal activity would need to be managed within the executive's policy functions. In spite of having very different foundations, both those advocating for post-colonial stability and those looking for an executive-led transition to communism were united in believing that an independent judiciary could undermine the implementation of executive policy.

Within this framework the judiciary is independent in the sense that its work is independent of other government bodies, which, for example, cannot remove a lawsuit from the consideration of the judiciary or modify a judgment passed by a court. Often this limited independence also includes judicial impunity different from that of other officials. Judges are officially only obliged in their work to obey the law; unlike other bureaucrats in the system they would not typically have policy obligations, such as increasing access to housing for the poor, imposed upon them. In consideration of this, and to accommodate concerns about maintaining impartiality, systems established for a judiciary maintained within the executive branch tend to enact laws to bestow guarantees intended to allow judges to perform their function properly. Interestingly, the guarantees are often worded very similarly to those outlined above for judges in an independent branch.

Dr. Thurwat Anees al-Seyoutti is a well-regarded advocate for maintaining the management of the judiciary within the umbrella of the executive. His opinion defines the judiciary not as an independent authority, but rather as a more limited state body whose function it is to administer the law and resolve disputes.[92] His position represents that of the Judicial Reformation Law, which

---

[92]   Judicial Reformation Law, No. 35 of 1977.

considers the judiciary independent in resolving disputes but still a state body participating in achieving the aims of the society as contained within government policy. He says "In a state, there is only one political power which draws up the general policy or the general framework of the society through legislation. There are two functions: administrative and judicial. Since there is only one power, this means there is no need for separation of power in the form of separate legislative, executive and judicial branches."[93]

Dr. Al-Seyoutti therefore views the functions of the judiciary in a manner similar to earlier systems pre-dating the full devolution of authority from central, all-powerful rulers. Although similar to historical structures, the rationale of academics such as Dr. al-Seyoutti is that with the decades of social change following WWII, the executive in many countries is an agent of positive social change. By extension, this group feels that the judiciary should be a tool for generating the positive social change defined by the executive. Dr. al-Seyoutti therefore does not want the judiciary to deviate from a policy path by interpreting the law in ways that would hinder the change to socialism. He even goes further when he says he wants the judiciary to give up its commitment to capitalist and the bourgeois classes and to adhere to the thoughts and goals of the revolutionary and socialist authorities. It should, he thinks, take a "legislative" role by issuing obligatory guidance from the High Court to all courts interpreting the laws in a revolutionary spirit to protect the gains made by the working class.[94]

To defend this view, he uses examples showing how the judiciary from France and America were antagonistic to the needs of the people and proved themselves to be committed to the bourgeois classes. A perfect example, he thinks, is the U.S. Supreme Court, which sided with the industrial capitalists against laborers by allowing clauses

---

[93]   Dr Thurwat Anees Al-Seyoutti, *Committed Judiciary* 1: 41.

[94]   Dr Thurwat Anees Al-Seyoutti, *Committed Judiciary* 1: 41.

unfavorable to workers to undermine the personal freedom which the U.S. Constitution nominally guaranteed. As for the French judiciary, Dr. al-Seyoutti dismissed its assertions of independence because there was a simple mechanism in place to ignore the judiciary's role in executive oversight when there was an emergency: "The semblance of great oversight is trivial in essence because it shrinks in emergencies."[95]

---

[95] *Id.* at 74.

CHAPTER SEVEN

Towards a Functional View of the Role of the Judiciary in a Modern Iraqi State

The above is an overview of key themes that have developed in Iraqi debates on judicial independence over the past several decades. Very important concepts have been debated, yet no consensus emerged that satisfied the critical test of functionality and Iraq has therefore seen one wave of governance approaches after another since the departure of the Ottomans. The theory of separation of power contends that governance is most effective when governance is divided into distinctly defined and supported powers. In most western democracies this concept has coalesced around three primary elements: the legislative, judicial, and executive branches. In order for this system to function each division needs to be independent of the others so that it can perform its mandate within boundaries established by the mandates and operations of the other divisions. The judiciary is concerned with applying the laws to cases or issues in line with constitutional and legislative frameworks. Administering justice necessitates resolving the conflicting interests of litigants, whatever their position or potential influence in society. If those who administer justice are not established independently, there is a risk created that they will not perform their mission objectively. According to the theory of separation of powers, the system is thereby weakened. In my opinion, as Iraq strives to affirm its modern state judicial independence is the most important pillar in any strategy for consolidating justice and the rule of law; it is what supports the translation of a theoretical "separation of powers" into a functional reality.

Thus the separation of powers in the constitution should not be viewed narrowly as an effort to empower judges. Rather, it is a critical part of making the machine designed by the constitution work to protect societal and individual freedoms. If we take the same case and outcome, but assess the implications under the systems discussed above, we have very different sets of considerations. For example, let us say that there is a contract case between a very rich person and a young farmer. One can imagine how both those advocating for the rich person, who has many connections and supports the ruling faction, and those advocating for the young farmer, perhaps extending Dr. al-Seyoutti's argument that judges should promote change for the proletariat, would both want the judge to skew his judgment. We may all have our sympathies and hopes for certain outcomes. Even if both systems resulted in the same outcome in an individual case, however, society is much better positioned when the case is decided by independent judges. Certainly both the businessman and the farmer would be equally disappointed if they lost their case. However with an independent judiciary the outcome is more likely to be trusted by society and respected by the losing party, and the case will not throw fear into all businessmen and all farmers that a new policy or law can threaten their rights under the constitution.

A system where the judiciary is part of the executive can leave losing parties adrift, while a system with independent judicial, legislative, and executive branches creates opportunities for people to test the application of new ideas. An independent judiciary is not one that is free to do what it likes; it is one where judges are free to apply the law fairly. Individuals can discuss with lawmakers changes to the law, or with the executive changes to regulations or enforcement if the courts are neutral arbiters of laws and application. Without the neutral arbiter, the system stalls because written laws and regulations become subservient to political whim. Regardless of the intent behind attempts to mold courts to policy, the effort weakens the potential for a vibrant democracy.

To that end, judicial independence plays an important role in consolidating the rule of law and delivery of justice. A law never applied is written in the sand. It is the fair application of the law that allows people to understand the importance of the legislature passing the law and the executive enforcing the law. Over time, the fair application of laws contributes greatly to what modern theorists call "state building", which in turn leads to development. It goes without saying that just as judges must be protected from intrusions from other branches, they, too, should avoid the temptations to engage in the work of the other branches. Put directly, judges should stay away from politics with its disputes and vicissitudes; they should maintain impartiality. The judiciary should be an authority to which the executive and legislative powers can resort to in disputes and for interpretation. An independent judiciary gains the confidence of the people and also of other branches. It does not discriminate between people, parties, or branches and should not come under any authority other than the law. Finally, a system built on the separation theory adapts. Laws and enforcement can expand, be refined, or be rescinded, as people apply pressure to the legislature or executive.

The above discussion outlines a number of arguments for an independent judiciary. In line with the above and the expositions of other authors, I suggest that there are a small number of core assurances that will provide independence for the judiciary. Given these, judges can occupy their constitutional positions and participate in building a community blessed with the rule of law. The critical elements of judicial independence are:

1- Clear and sound regulations are needed to show how judges are appointed, given salary increases, promoted, transferred, and retired. In Iraq, this means that a judge should never be appointed, have his salary raised, be transferred, or be retired without following the procedure set in the Judicial Organization

Law. Any action related to a judge should be carried out by a judicial body without any intervention from any power or party.

2- As a neutral actor applying a law, a judge should not be held individually responsible for the judgments they pass. In applying the law, there are many situations where parties can be injured. As discussed above, parties or groups can advocate for new laws or other changes but the court is not the correct time to expect change. Of course, if the judgment came as a result of deception or serious professional error a higher judicial body should carry out the investigation and the complainant should follow the litigation procedure set up by the law.

3- Financial independence of the judiciary. One distinctive feature of judicial independence is a budget independent of the executive power. Historically, the judiciary is the point of friction between the legislature and the executive as the laws passed by one can become irksome to the other. Allowing the executive to choke the vital flow of resources to the judiciary hurts individuals, undermines the legislature who will not be able to independently enforce their laws, and can even put judicial actors at risk of serious harm. Linking the judiciary budget to a ministry or any other body renders it subordinate to that ministry, restricting its freedom of action. Yemen emphasizes in Article (147) of its constitution the principle of the financial independence of the judiciary: "The judiciary is a judicially and financial independent power." Of course, there will be general accounting standards and budget processes that the judicial branch must follow like any other government body. That is a separate discussion. On their part, jurists think the aim of the financial independence of the judiciary is to protect it "from the flightiness of government and foes."[96]

---

[96] Mohammed Said Al-Ashmawi and Abdul Wahaab Al-Ashmawi, *Procedural Rules* at 31; Dr Ahmed Abu al-Wafa, *Hearings in Civil and Commercial Cases*, 5th ed., 56.

CHAPTER EIGHT

Judicial Organization Law
No. 160 of 1977

Let's return to the Judicial Organization Law— the topic of this part—to see where it stood regarding judicial independence and its provisions in this respect. Some initial queries are suggested by our discussion to this point: Has the law set enough guarantees to ensure judicial independence in line with those listed above? Does it appropriately establish and support the status necessary for an independent Iraqi judiciary? Historically, the Iraqi judiciary built a reputation for independent thinking, neutrality, the search for justice, and proactive adaptation of new techniques, methodology and learning. To some extent, the historical structure can be credited for this as the civil law system borrowed by the Ottomans from the French allows judges a great deal of leeway in exploring both the evidence and the arguments presented to provide context for the evidence. Individual determination must also be credited, however, as there were certainly times of extreme pressure on the judges of Iraq during its history where various actors and forces would prefer less independent review of cases.

As background to our review of this law, I note that the Provisional Constitution issued on July 14, 1970 stipulated that judicial independence was a fundamental principle for the new constitution. It also detailed the method of courts formation, levels and jurisdiction of courts, requirements for judicial appointments, salary increases, conditions for transfer, standards of accountability, and guidelines for retirement.[97] From 1970-1977, therefore, the judicial profession in Iraq evolved fully committed to the principle of judicial independence at all levels and in both civil and criminal courts. Within the systems of the time there were assurances to ensure that a judge applied the law fairly and humanely without concern that any professional or personal harm would befall them.

The Judicial Oversight Law, No. 124 of 1979 (1979 Oversight Law) further expanded this principle because it entrusted the judicial supervisors, who were also judges, with the task of overseeing and inspecting courts and judges' administrative and judicial work. This was a break from previous practices where colonial or executive authorities would perform this task, creating potential areas for manipulation of judges or interference with cases. The provision also increased the sophistication of the analysis of performance as judges could be held to a higher standard by other judges, just as a surgeon's work would benefit more from review by another surgeon rather than by an accountant.

The contemporary legal framework also created a well-defined platform for the jurisdiction of Iraqi courts. Civil Procedure Law No. 83 of 1969 stated that the jurisdiction of the judiciary covers all persons whether natural or legal (i.e. corporations), including the government, and confirmed that courts had authority to "resolve all legal disputes."[98] The Civil Procedure Law also called for the respect of all legal judgments and made them valid until they were repealed

---

[97] Article (63) of the Provisional Constitution of Iraq states:
The judiciary is independent and does not come under any power other than the law;
All citizens have the right to litigate.

[98] Article (29) of the Civil Procedure Law states: "The jurisdiction of civil courts shall apply to all natural or juristic persons including the government, and shall be specialized in resolving all disputes except those excluded by law".

or amended by law.[99] Penalty Law No. 111 of 1969 bolstered these acts to further emphasize judicial independence. It precluded any intervention in court procedure with penalties for any interference "for or against a litigant."[100] Note that the drafting followed the unfortunate practice of including specific fine amounts within the law itself rather than allowing administrative adjustments as a regulatory matter.

This law bears looking into in more detail to see how it impacts judicial independence in practice.

1. Provisions governing the work of the Federal Court of Cassation

The Court of Cassation was the highest judicial institution in Iraq before the formation of the Federal Supreme Court in 2005. The 1977 Organization Law gave the Chief Justice of the Court of Cassation the power to manage and organize the court's procedures. It also established a Presidential Panel consisting of the Chief Justice and his deputies to select members of the judicial commissions. Although a step towards judicial independence, the 1979 Oversight Law required annual reports from the Chief Justice to the Minister of Justice and Justice Council.[101] Illustrating our discussion above about the various ends used to justify the means of curtailing judicial independence, the Ministry of Justice's Organic Law empowers the Minister to hold seminars and meetings with the judges, including judges of the Cassation Court, to ensure that the

---

[99]   Article (3-160) of the Civil Procedure Law states: "A judgment passed by a court shall remain valid and considered unless it is revoked or amended by the court itself or overruled or overturned by a higher court according to the law."

[100] Article (33) of the Penal Law states: "A penalty not exceeding one year imprisonment or a fine not exceeding one hundred dinars shall be imposed on any government official or any individual charged with public service who intercedes on behalf of or against one litigant."

[101] Judicial Organization Law of 1977, Article 55 (1) C.

goals of the Party and the Revolution are fulfilled.[102] These two articles show that the executive power could infringe upon the independence of the courts by allowing direct channels for the application of policy pressures on judges.

2. Provisions governing the work of the Federal Appellate Courts

The Organization Law of 1977 charged the Chief Justice of each Appellate Court District with the task of overseeing the courts and their work within the appellate district, including assigning judges to duties.[103]

The law set up a council in every appellate district to address problems and challenges facing the courts. Chaired by the Chief Justice of the Appellate Court and supported with their deputies, the committees were empowered to refine procedures and tasked with improving performance.[104]

Although the Court of Cassation was linked to the executive through the operation of the Justice Ministry's Organic Law, the appellate courts are directly linked to executive oversight in the Organization Law. Article 18 charged the Minister of Justice with oversight over all

---

[102] Ministry of Justice Law Article 1-2. Editor's Note: year of law undefined by the translators, but presumed to be between 1977-79.

[103] Article (18) of the Judicial Organization Law states: "The Chief Justice of an Appellate Court shall supervise the courts and their work within his Appellate area and distribute the work among judges. He is empowered to mandate one of his deputies to take over any of his powers he thinks appropriate."

[104] Article (19) of the Judicial Organization Law states: "First: In every appellate area a council chaired by the Chief Justice of the Appellate Court with membership of Deputies of the Chief Justice and members of the Appellate Court. This council is called the Council of (Governorate' name) Appellate Area."

courts and judges, including the review of their personal and formal conduct.

3. Provisions governing judges' affairs

The Judicial Organization Law mandated the creation of a committee consisting of three judges the Justice Council selected from its members at the beginning of each year.[105] Articles 3-4 of the Ministry of Justice Law No. 101 of 1977 outlines the procedures for initiating a case against a judge under either the Judicial Organization Law or the older Judicial Authority Law from 1963.[106] In general, the Minister of Justice initiated cases against judges by filing a complaint with the committee.[107] The committee would review the submission of both the ministry and the accused in terms of measures set by the law. These measures guaranteed defense for the judge concerned and made the committee's decision subject to legal challenge (by either the accused judge or the ministry) before a plenary session of the Court of Cassation.

---

[105] Article (60) of the Judicial Organization Law states: "First: A disciplinary action against a judge is initiated on a decision of the Minister of Justice referring the concerned judge to the Judges' Affairs Committee, detailing the offence he is alleged to have committed and related proofs. A copy of this decision is sent to the judge concerned and the public prosecutor."

[106] Article (3-4) of the Ministry of Justice Law states: "A committee shall be formed, called the Judges' and Qadis' Affairs Committee, consisting of three judges the Justice Council selects from its members at the beginning of each year to resolve disputes and take disciplinary actions against judges and *qadis* in terms of provisions of Chapter Eight of Law No. 26 of 1963. It also looks into cases arising from its provisions. The committee decision is subject to legal challenge at the General Assembly of the Court of Cassation by the Minister of Justice and by the judge ruled against within thirty days as of the date of notification. The General Assembly decision is irrevocable."

[107] Judicial Organization Law, Article 60/1.

The principle that a judge is investigated and tried disciplinarily in matters related to his profession by a judicial committee is very old. Iraq's Judicial Organization Law and Judicial Authority Law were therefore similar in structure and intent to judicial oversight laws in many other countries.[108] However, Iraqi law diverged from other countries by empowering only the Minister of Justice, but not a judicial committee, to refer a judge to the committee.[109] Some view this mechanism as creating a healthy external check on the judicial branch, yet the restriction of the power of review to *only* the Ministry of Justice meant that the judiciary itself was not able to review the neutrality of its members. This limitation was heavily felt in later years as political pressures on the judiciary grew.

The above-mentioned provisions show clearly that judicial independence must be considered in light of the prevailing political perspectives at the time. In the 1970's, the political authorities were primarily coming from a perspective that the judiciary and, to a large extent, the legislative branch, should further the policy aims of the executive. They therefore did not promote the separation of powers as modern readers may understand the concept. In reality, authorities at the time often did their utmost to isolate institutions from the democratic influence of society. Rather than empowering the people within the country, the state was intent on applying its force to shape society in line with its ideology. This was in line with Marxist trends in many parts of the world.

During the time period between the abolition of the Judicial Council in 1977 and its reinstitution in 2003 after the downfall of Saddam Hussein, judges suffered a great deal performing their duties. The harassment took many forms, but typically used tools that made a judge fear for either their own or their family's well-being. Judges out of favor with the executive faced unjustified transfers, transfer out

---

[108] Judicial Authority Law, No. 26 of 1963, Articles (57-59).

[109] Judicial Organization Law, Article (60/First).

of the judiciary to a post in the civil service, dismissal, disbarment from the legal profession, and even imprisonment. Moreover, the executive control over the judicial profession resulted in a situation where people qualified in law were not allowed to take up judicial posts because they did not hold the trust of the regime. Conversely, unqualified people were promoted into the judiciary in order to effect changes desired by the executive. The provisions only allowing only the Minister of Justice to review the performance of judges had far-reaching consequences during this period.

The abolition of the Judicial Council and creation of an executive-controlled Justice Council in 1977 was a particularly dangerous development in the history of justice in Iraq. It hurt individual judges and struck a blow to democratic growth by undermining judicial independence since the Justice Council was chaired by the Minister of Justice. These sentences are not an indictment of the people that hold the title of Minister of Justice, many of whom have been very righteous people. It is the system itself that is being assessed. Regardless of how sublime the individual holding a position is, they cannot overcome the negative force created by an unbalanced system. The result is unjust for the people, and unfair to both judges and to the person forced to sit as minister if the constitutional mandate to establish an independent judiciary is to be fulfilled. Indeed, the position of minister is explicitly established to develop and further executive policy. If the person in that post did any less, even if some preferred that action because it supported the judiciary in a particular instance, the minister would in fact still be undermining the separation of powers by not performing their executive function to the best of their ability.

More often ministers have been obligated to apply negative pressures to the judiciary in furtherance of government (executive) interests. We have several examples of this problem arising in lawsuits involving the government where the Justice Council gave instructions, either directly or implicitly, that government interests should be advanced. In this respect, I personally remember a Minister of Justice, in a meeting of the Justice Council, saying that he would evict an entire court from a house it was renting if the judge passed a particular sentence. With regard to this rental, note that even today courts in Iraq have had to find creative ways to bring justice to places accessible to the community. Since the executive and legislative branches maintain many budgetary and administrative controls over the judicial branch, funding for courts and staff remains extremely limited. In response, the judiciary has done its best to respond to community requests for courts by using temporary systems, including the rental of large houses and compounds to be used as courts. The Minister's threat to the judge forced the judge to not only consider his own well-being, but also the access of a large community to a court of law. Undoubtedly the order of the Judicial Council in this case constituted a violation of judicial impartiality. The impact of these types of orders can be seen in the rise of extreme executive authority in the decades following the passage of the 1977 law. Furthermore, the Minister of Justice, being chair of the Justice Council, was able to exert pressure on judges by threatening their career or family well-being through administrative powers granted to the Council. Judicial transfer approvals, salary increases, promotions, and even the initial posting of judges were all decision assigned to the Justice Council by the Judicial Organization Law.

As mentioned, not all ministers were adverse to the rule of law and antagonistic to fair conditions for judges. The Justice Council's policy changed with each change of the Minister of Justice, affecting either positively or negatively judges' conditions and affairs. The summer does not make the winter less harsh, however, so a house must be built that can stand strong regardless of the weather. Therefore a stand should be taken to ensure that the modern state institutes enough legal and regulatory guarantees to safeguard real judicial independence given Iraq's long history with different models.

PART 3

Modern Iraqi Judicial & Court Systems

CHAPTER NINE

The Re-establishment of the Judicial Council

Through the 1980s and 1990s, judges in Iraq and others interested in judicial independence kept calling for the re-establishment of a (judicially-controlled) Judicial Council to take care of the affairs of judges and public prosecutors independently from the executive. These calls became louder after the change of regime in Iraq on April 9, 2003, the date the tyrannical system collapsed after it ruled Iraq for over three decades.

The older Justice – differentiated from a *Judicial* – Council, whatever form it took, was subordinated to the executive power because the Minister of Justice chaired it. Given the Minister's mandatory obligation to promote policy within the executive branch, all matters pertaining to judges and members of the public prosecution were indirectly in the hands of the executive power. Subjugating the Judicial Council, which should be both the symbol and tool of neutral justice for all under the Constitution, to the executive power contradicts the constitutional provisions which govern powers and leaves the system itself dysfunctional for those most in need.

Taken to extremes, the lack of a duly powered independent judiciary will leave the most desperate in society without recourse under the Constitution. For judicial independence to succeed, every party, both governing and governed, must believe in it. This change in thinking is required to guarantee rights, establish liberties, and to provide a foundation stone for the public trust needed for a modern economic system.

In light of this, the Transitional Provisional Authority promulgated Order No. 35 of 2003 (Order No. 35) to re-establish a Judicial Council in Iraq. Its preamble itself begins with a call for an independent judiciary: "The key to the establishment of the rule of law is a judicial system staffed by capable persons and free and independent from outside influences."[110] Thus the aim is crystal clear—it is the establishment of an independent judicial branch that can fulfil democratic mandates aspired to since independence in Iraq. Note that Order No. 35 operated alongside the Judicial Authority Law No. 160 of 1979 and the Public Prosecution Law No. 159 of 1979 where these two laws did not conflict with the new Order.

With Order No. 35, Iraq achieved two gains: First, the re-establishment of a judicially-controlled Judicial Council to be responsible for supervising the judicial system and courts in Iraq independently of the Ministry of Justice; Second, the advancement towards creating a properly functioning third branch of government that could, with the executive and legislative branches, build a sustainable state based on the rule of law in Iraq. With the re-establishment of the Judicial Council, the legislature affirmed support for the reformed Judicial Council's authority to oversee the work of judges and members of the public prosecution away from intervening influences.

This was confirmed by Part Six of Order No. 35, which stated that the Judicial Council should exercise its tasks and responsibilities independently of supervision from the Ministry of Justice and that any provision in any law contradicting this independence was repealed. The Judicial Council re-established by Order 35 replaced the Justice Council formed by Ministry of Justice Law No (101) of

---

[110]   Transitional Provisional Authority Order No. 35 of 2003.

1977; judges and public prosecutors therefore worked independently of the executive power beginning in 2003. Given proper legislative and administrative support, this meant that the judiciary could work without influence of any political party, and without fear of administrative penalties or hurdles such as the fear of being transferred or having their salary increase or promotion delayed. Order 35 also created an opportunity to move away from judges being punished, dismissed, or imprisoned without cause since the Order meant that the judicial supervising authority should consist of fellow judges.

Order 35 established a Judicial Council consisting of the actors responsible for all judicial matters. Chaired by the Chief Justice of the Cassation Court, the Council included the five Deputy Chief Justices of the Cassation Court, the President of the State Consultative Council, the Chief Public Prosecutor, Chairman of the Legal Oversight Commission, the Director General of the Administrative unit if such a person is a judge or a public prosecutor, and the Chief Justices of the Appellate Courts, of which there were fourteen at the time. The Order also confirmed a number of employees under the command of the Council Secretary General.

Order 35 further detailed the tasks of the Judicial Council in Part Three:

- Complete administrative supervision on matters relating to judges and public prosecutors, with the exception of members of the Cassation Court, which are supervised by the Chief Justice in accordance with the Judicial Authority Law;[111]

---

[111] Judicial Authority Law No. 160 of 1979.

- Nomination of qualified candidates to judicial posts specified in the Judicial Organization Law and Public Prosecution Law;

- Managing judicial and prosecutor promotions, salary increases, assignments, and transfers;

- Investigating allegations of improper conduct against judges and prosecutors and disciplining any found guilty.

Order No. 35 pre-dated the modern Iraqi Constitution by several years, and left the door open to the creation of additional obligations for the Judicial Council. By 2003, however, we can already say that the judiciary was intended to run its own affairs without intervention. For added clarification, Order No. 35 further stated that: "the Council performs its functions independently of the Ministry of Justice," that "the Council shall exercise its functions independently of any scrutiny or supervision from the Ministry of Justice."[112]

In furtherance of this mandate, the Judicial Council worked in early days to build the administrative structure that history showed was essential for stable, independent judicial functions. Due to a number of factors, small, but critical elements, such as budgets and staffing, were not fully addressed in 2003 and the early efforts of the Judicial Council were heavily burdened by having to work through these issues with successive executive and international partners. By 2009, the Judicial Council had established its own budget, offices, and property[113] to oversee the management of all judicial and court staff other than some elements of security, which remains a significant concern through the present time.

---

[112] TPA Order No. 35 of 2003, Section 1-3, 6.

[113] The Higher Judicial Council was given the right to own property, whether chattel or immovable, as per Legislative Order No. 12 of 2004.

All these transformations in Iraqi Judicial System were later also embodied in Part Three of the Law of Administration for the State of Iraq for the Transitional Period, which was passed in 2004. This law further affirmed that the Judicial Council's budget is approved by the National Assembly (legislative branch) as opposed to the Ministry of Finance (executive branch), that a judge should not be dismissed unless indicted for a crime of disgrace or corruption, and that judicial salaries could not be reduced or held for any reason.[114] Additional guidance was also given on the intent of the drafters to create a tripartite separation of powers, including an independent judiciary, with the explicit belief that this effort would contribute to increased stability and citizen oversight over the government.[115]

In earlier discussions we explored the rationale for judicial independence. Following the 2003 and 2004 efforts to create the Judicial Council, debate again flared about the need for, and scope of, judicial independence. While many inside and outside Iraq rallied behind international principles supporting judicial independence, it was also clear that some international and Iraqi actors were not comfortable with the full impact of independence. The Council advocated for growth based solely on an understanding of history and on the governance theory that the separation of powers results in a healthier, more stable system. Others were concerned about short term delays to international or government programs or, perhaps, intimidated by the creation of a new body during such a violent and confusing time.

---

[114] Law of Administration for the State of Iraq during the Transitional Period, Article (47).

[115] The evolution of judicial independence is discussed above, and further support emerged in UN General Assembly Resolutions No (40/32) of Nov 29, 1985 and No (40/46) of Dec 29, 1985, which cover the main principles of judicial independence and the means to achieve it; Beirut Declaration for Justice issued by the First Arab Conference on Justice; and the <u>Cairo Declaration on Judicial Independence</u> in Arab Countries issued by the Second Arab Conference on Justice in 2003.

By 2004, Iraq and its partners had shifted to discussions about new Constitution required to support Iraq's return to sovereign status. For historical purposes, I outline some of the principles relating to the judiciary that emerged from these discussions:

1. The judiciary should be independent, operate within its mandate on a par with the executive and legislative powers, and, with the other two branches, create a modern tripartite state. Accordingly, only the judiciary should have jurisdiction over disputes between both natural and juristic, including corporations and the government, parties, with due consideration to international conventions in this respect;

2. The judiciary should be the only power that deals with matters relating to judges, members of the public prosecution, and institutions, such as courts, the Judicial Development Institute, and others beholden to them. In no way can the executive and legislative powers meddle in its business beyond the scope of constitutional checks and balances, such as budgetary review afforded to the legislative branch. Anyone trying to intercede should be liable for prosecution;

3. The Chief Justice of the judiciary should report directly to the President of the Republic, being the representative of the state, to emphasize the independence of the judiciary from the executive and legislative branches;

4. The judiciary shall have its own legal identity for the purposes of all operational matters, including property ownership and transfer, and financial and administrative independence through a well-defined, but independent budget process and its own dedicated staffing structure. Given the unique nature of Iraq following the fall of the former regime, the judiciary should be given full support for establishing its own security structures. The budget should

be submitted directly to the Parliament for approval, thus confirming judicial independence;

5. The judicial branch should be the only authority to specify the measures followed by courts and judicial institutions in resolving disputes;

6. The sentences and rulings passed by courts and judicial institutions beholden to the judiciary should be unreservedly binding and the executive agencies should be bound to execute them as necessary. Anyone refraining from implementing within all due care and speed shall be subject to prosecution;

7. The appointment, management and discipline of judges, including prosecutors, be a responsibility restricted only to the judicial branch;

8. Any amendment to judiciary-related constitutional provisions or related laws should be carried out after consultation with the judiciary.

These principles emerged from our review of Iraq's history and addressed problems that previous laws had created or left unresolved. We will discuss how constitutional and legislative processes captured recommendations in subsequent sections. We should now turn to Law of Administration for the State of Iraq for the Transitional Period (Law for the Transitional Period), which was in essence a provisional constitution defining the direction of the modern Iraqi state pending the completion of the 2005 Constitution.

Part Six of the Law for the Transitional Period was titled "Federal Judicial Authority." It set out the general guidelines for judicial and court organization in Iraq with few details. In Clause (A) of Article 43, it stipulated "[t]he judiciary is independent and is not directed by the executive power including the Ministry of Justice." The Law also stated that the judiciary exercised its jurisdiction with no intervention by either the legislative or executive powers.

The same article divided the courts into two types: federal courts and regional courts. In Article 46, the Law for the Transitional Period defined the federal courts as simply those courts existing outside of the Kurdistan region. The Cassation Court in Baghdad sat at the top of this structure, with Appellate Courts maintained within court districts to manage subsidiary courts within the districts. These courts were given jurisdiction over the application of federal laws. The Law defined regional courts as those within the Kurdistan region applying regional laws.

Importantly, the Law for the Transitional Period was silent as to linkages or relationships between regional and federal courts. Many believed that this matter, along with other details on jurisdiction, administration, and supervision, would be addressed through Organic legislation or related regulations. Earlier versions of this work anticipated this legislation would quickly follow the passage of the Constitution. Indeed, the Judicial Council did complete its preparation for the legislation. Unfortunately, one additional element was also missing from the Law for the Transitional Period and the Constitution: clarity on how the Judicial Council could contribute to the new legislation in light of its new status within a new branch of government. The history and current status of this legislation is discussed in more detail in the Addendum to the Introduction preceding Chapter 1 of this book.

*Chief Justice with the Special Investigator General for Iraq
Reconstruction, Stuart Bowen – Date Unknown*

The Law for the Transitional Period amended the TPA Order No. 35 by changing the title of the Judicial Council to the Higher Judicial Council (HJC) and created a Federal Supreme Court in addition to the Cassation Court. The Chief Justice of the Federal Supreme Court was, by extension, also the President of the Higher Judicial Council. Every head of a Court of Appeal also became a member of the Higher Judicial Council. According to Article 45 of the law, the Chief Justice of the Supreme Court would be elected by a secret ballot in a plenary session of Higher Judicial Council to take the Chair of the HJC, while the Chief Justice of the Court of Cassation would become the Vice President of the HJC. It is worthwhile to mention that the position of President of the Higher Judicial Council required sufficient experience, technical competence and management skills to effectively deploy and support more than one thousand judges, and many more thousands in court staff and security, throughout a large country like Iraq. Many other countries in the region, including Jordan, Syria and Kuwait, also have the head of the highest Court in the nation lead administrative and oversight bodies similar to the HJC so this model is well established in the region. All of the senior positions in the court system—the Chief Justice of the Federal Court of Cassation, the Chief Justices of Appellate Courts, the Chief Prosecutor and the Chairman of Judicial Oversight

Commission – require a rare level of skill, experience, and values and the latitude to apply these qualities independently. These position cannot be appropriately managed through mechanisms that can be manipulated by political or sectarian considerations. In fact, if the judiciary is to play a societal role in maintaining a neutral space for different factions to engage fairly with each other, it is essential that all aspects of judicial selection and management be isolated from even the appearance of political or sectarian bias.

The 2005 Constitution confirmed the status and position of the Higher Judicial Council, with a final membership of: the Chief Justice of the Federal Supreme Court as chairman; the Chief Justice of Federal Cassation Court and his deputies; Chief Justices of Federal Appellate Courts; the Chief Justice of Court of Cassation for Kurdistan and his two deputies; and the Chief Public Prosecutor and Chief Justice of Judicial Oversight Commission. Following the 2005 Constitution,[116] and pending expected subsequent legislation, the HJC was empowered to supervise the judiciary and courts in general, while a regional council in the Kurdistan Region of Iraq was responsible for the appointment, transfer, promotion, and retirement of judges and members of the public prosecution in the region.

Our review shows a healthy understanding of what is needed in Iraq to provide a legitimate, independent court system that can meet the expectations of a democratic society. Since 2003, there has been an important Order re-establishing an independent judicial management body, the Law of the Transitional Period that created a Higher Judicial Council to tie in lessons learned from other Arab States, and the 2005 Constitution, which created the moral and structural foundation for a fully independent judiciary for the first time in Iraq's history through Articles 19 and 87. Looking forward, there is clear momentum for the Higher Judicial Council to operate without any intervention so that it can play its pioneering role in creating a state based on the rule of law.

---

[116] Constitution of the Republic of Iraq, Article (93), 2005.

CHAPTER TEN

The Federal Courts Supported Through the Higher Judicial Council

Section A. Federal Supreme Court

A Sitting of the Federal Supreme Court

Perhaps reflecting similar gaps in the governance structures of successive colonial powers, the nation of Iraq never created a court authorized to resolve disputes regarding the constitutionality of laws, resolutions, orders, and regulations issued by the legislative and executive powers. The resulting 'judicial vacuum' reflected negatively on the rights of the people and rule of law. The sitting judiciary in Iraq was blocked from considering issues of constitutionality by clear civil law principles limiting the judiciary to strictly apply laws within the scope of their jurisdiction. The judiciary often ran into conflict with the executive power in its attempt to hear cases on the illegality of some laws or resolutions which have the power of a law.

Therefore, when the modern state was reviewing constitutional issues in 2004 many recognized the need for a high court with the jurisdiction to ensure respect for constitutional provisions, enhance the principle of rule of law and to stop the legislature or the executive power from transgressing the basic principles or constitutional provisions fundamental to the state. Article 44 of the Law of the Transitional Period established Federal Supreme Court in Iraq.

Law No. 30 of 2005, the Law of Federal Supreme Court, was gazetted in March 2005. Article 1 of this Law stipulated "[a] court named the Federal Supreme Court shall be set up and shall have its headquarters in Baghdad. It shall operate independently and not come under any power other than the law." Clauses B and C of Article 44 of the Law of the Transitional Period defined the functions of the Federal Supreme Court as:

1. Resolve disputes arising between government actors, i.e. within or between the federal government, governments of regions, provinces, municipalities and local administrations;

2. At the request of a court, a government department, or an individual claimant, resolve disputes over the constitutionality of laws, resolutions, orders, and regulations issued by a body authorized to pass them;

3. Review legal challenges against rulings of the Administrative Court;

4. Sit as an Appellate Court on cases appealed within a jurisdiction established by subsidiary legislation.[117]

In Article 93, the Constitution of the Republic of Iraq of 2005 defined the jurisdiction of Supreme Federal Court as follows:

1. Assess the constitutionality of laws and regulations;

2. Interpret constitutional provisions on request;

3. Resolve cases arising from the application of federal laws, regulations, instructions and measures. The Constitution provided the right for legal challenges to both government and individuals;

4. Resolve disputes arising between and among government levels, including federal government, regional government, provinces, municipalities and local administrations;

5. Resolve accusations made against the President of the Republic, the Prime Minister, or Ministers;

6. Approve the final results of the parliamentary general elections;

7. Resolve disputes between the federal judiciary and courts in regions and courts in provinces not affiliated to regions;

8. Settle disputes over jurisdiction among provinces not affiliated to regions.

---

[117] Note that this obligation was de jure only at the time as it required the passage of legislation to fully describe, and create practical systems for exercising, this jurisdiction.

The second clause of Article 52 also expanded the jurisdiction of the Federal Supreme Court to the resolution of challenges to qualifications for a Member of Parliament if the challenge was submitted within thirty days of the passage of a resolution in question. Subsequent legislation added further obligations to the Federal Supreme Court, suggesting a growing comfort with the body as a means of neutrally resolving contentious issues. For example, the Nationality Law No. 26 of 2006 tasked the Federal Supreme Court with reviewing challenges to Ministry of Interior decisions to withhold Iraq nationality from an applicant.

Article 89 of the Constitution of the Republic of Iraq of 2005 described the Judicial Authority of Iraq as consisting of the Federal Supreme Court, the Higher Judicial Council, the Federal Court of Cassation, the Public Prosecution System, the Judicial Oversight Commission, and other Federal Courts which are governed by law. Article 94 of the Constitution stipulated that rulings of the Federal Supreme Court are binding on all authorities. This legal power targeted the creation of a stable legal system and sustained rule of law, resulting in protection of both rights and freedoms.

By operation of the Constitution, the Federal Supreme Court is made up of nine members. The Higher Judicial Council, after consultation with Regional Higher Judicial Councils, was charged with nominating eighteen to twenty-seven candidates to fill initial vacancies in the Federal Supreme Court. For any subsequent vacancy resulting from death, retirement or dismissal, the HJC was required to nominate three candidates. The former Presidency Council, and now the President, was charged with selecting members from the shortlist provided by the HJC. If any candidate was flatly rejected by the President, the Higher Judicial Council was required to nominate another three candidates.[118]

---

[118] This is stated in Item (E) of the Law of Administration for the State of Iraq for the Transitional Period, 2004; Law of the Federal Supreme Court, Law No. 30 of 2005.

Based on these provisions, the Higher Judicial Council nominated 27 candidates for the initial Federal Supreme Court on July 7, 2004 in a secret ballot. Careful consideration was given to experience levels, competence, and ability to continue service given a number of factors. The list of candidates with the tallied score against each name together with their CVs was then sent to the Presidency Council, which then deliberated with select advisors present. The process took more than six months, however in late March, 2005 Presidential Decree No (67) was issued. The Decree named Iraq's first Federal Supreme Court:

- Madhat Hamoudi Al-Mahmood, the Chief Justice;

- Abud Salih Al-Timimi;

- Jaafir Nassir Hussein;

- Ahmed Al-Jaleeli;

- Farouk Ahmed Al-Sammi;

- Akram Taha Ahmed;

- Maikhael Shamshun Kes Korkes;

- Akram Ahmed Babaan;

- Muhammed Saeb Al-Nakshabindi.

Presidential Decree No. 2 of 2005 affirmed the appointment of the Chief Justice and members of Supreme Federal Court listed in Presidential Decree No. 67 of 2005. After the formation of the National Government and in view of retirement for medical reasons of a justice of Supreme Federal Court, a Presidential Decree No. 3 of 2007 appointed Justice Hussein Abu Al-Temin as his replacement. To ensure that the Court operated smoothly, Presidential decree No.

61 of 2009 named two justices from the Federal Cassation Court as standby judges on the Federal Supreme Court in addition to their duties on the Federal Cassation Court. They were Justices Khalil Ibrahim Khalefa (now retired) and Sami Hussein Al-Mamuri. These seemingly banal developments demonstrate that the system was well received by the broader government of Iraq, including the Presidency Council, was able to be adapted to meet critical needs by taking steps such as nominating stand-by judges, and could operate smoothly through the change of government generated through a relatively peaceful election cycle.

As with other aspects of the Judicial Authority, the 2005 Constitution anticipated organic laws that would better define and develop institutions such as the Federal Supreme Court created by the Constitution. The Higher Judicial Council prepared many academic and technical papers to inform this process, including a suggested draft Law of the Federal Supreme Court. These contributions took into consideration expert opinions from national and international contributors, historical and technical analysis, and other variables which arose from the enforcement of Law No. 30 of 2005. Due to the constitution's silence on how the laws mandated by the Constitution were going to be drafted, however, the HJC's contributions were insufficient in and of themselves to generate the necessary momentum. The drafts were sent to Parliament for consideration, but there has only been the confused movement outlined in the Addendum to the Introduction. Sadly, this is insufficient to support the promise of an independent judiciary.

Organizationally, the Federal Supreme Court consists of Directorates General of Administration, Finance, and Legal Affairs. Each is headed by a director general and contains the following departments:

1- Cases

2- Administrative and Financial

3- Secretariat

The Higher Judicial Council ensures that all of its units adhere to the highest possible financial standards. To this end, the IFIMS system has been adopted to enter all expenditure and revenues of the budget in the national database before anything is transferred into records. The roll-out of the system included joint training with executive actors to ensure that court staff were able to maintain data and produce reports. Further, their skills have been used to establish a library with legal reference materials cataloged for research and loan.

From the time it starting operating to the end of 2009, the Supreme Federal Court has received the following cases:

Year	No. of Cases	No. Cassation Cases	No. of Consultation Given
2005	3	36	None
2006	21	40	3
2007	15	23	17
2008	33	82	13
2009	48	122	33

Although the growth of the reliance on the court was heartening on many levels, indicating a renewed faith in the need for a judicial branch and trust in the outcomes of a neutral arbiter, the move from 39 total cases in 2005 to more than 200 in 2009 was very challenging. In addition to needing to establish brand new administrative systems without clear legislative or regulatory systems in place, the Federal Supreme Court was heavily lobbied by the range of political actors struggling to meet the needs of their constituents in a complicated – and often violent – atmosphere. But the court judges, believing in the importance of their promising role and remaining constant in their determination to make the Federal Supreme Court succeed in consolidating the provisions and principles of the constitution and in enforcing the rule of law, providing unbroken service to the people of Iraq.

Section B. Federal Cassation Court

Article 12 of the historic Judicial Organization Law created the Federal Cassation Court as the highest court in Iraq with a responsibility for supervising all the other courts. This must currently be interpreted in line with the provisions of the Law of the Transitional Period and the Constitution of 2005, of course. The Court of Cassation consists of a Chief Justice, five deputies to the Chief Justice and at least thirty five justices. Its headquarters is in Baghdad. This Court was originally set up long before the Judicial Organization Law, and actually dates back to a Royal Decree issued in 1925.

Articles 35, 203, and 216 of the Civil Procedure Law No. 83 of 1969 gave the jurisdiction of the Cassation Court as follows:

o To review challenges against rulings and resolutions: issued by Appellate Courts in their capacity as such; those of Courts of First Instance which are directed on appeal to the Cassation Court; that are handed down by Personal Status Courts, including Personal Status Courts for Non-Moslems;

• To consider all the issues that laws stipulate the Court of Cassation look into in its cassation capacity;[119]

• To examine all sentences which are by law subject to cassation challenge whether lodged by the parties concerned or not, provided the issue lies in the civil or criminal domain.[120]

---

[119] Madhat Al- Mahmood, *Explanation of Civil Procedure Law No (83) of 1969*, Part One, 61.

[120] Article (309) of the Civil Hearing Law; Article (254) of the Civil Procedure Law, No. 23 of 1971; Article (16) of the Public Prosecution Law, No. 159 of 1979.

The Court of Cassation is not regarded as a step within the core litigation process. In fact, it is review and monitoring body that does not normally hold hearings on the facts of a case. However, the court can rule on the facts of a case if, on review, the relevant unit decides that the case should be resolved after a sentence under review is overturned.[121] In this case, the sentence it hands down would be subject to challenge through the sentence rectification process at the Cassation Court's General Assembly.

This Court is run by a Chief Justice and has its separate budget. The work within the Court is distributed by the Presidential Committee consisting of the Chief Justice, his deputies and a senior justice if one deputy is absent. The Court is completely independent within its area of jurisdiction. The Court of Cassation is composed of a number of commissions which ensure it accomplishes its purpose as efficiently as possible. Their number is based on specialization in one or more case types, and evolved through 1979 when the commissions were outlined in Article 13 of the Judicial Organization Law No. 116:

1:   The General Assembly

This commission is presided over by the Chief Justice or a senior Deputy Chief Justice when the Chief Justice is absent or cannot attend for a legally justified reason. Its members include all Deputy Chief Justices and all justices sitting in the Court. It deals with:

1- Issues referred to the General Assembly by commissions that are considering abandoning a previously established principle;

2- Judgments which carry a death sentence;

---

[121]   Article (214) of the Civil Procedure Law.

3- Resolving disputes over contradiction in judgments between resolutions passed by the Federal Court of Cassation.

2: Expanded Civil Commission

This commission is presided over by the Chief Justice or a senior Deputy Chief Justice when the Chief Justice is absent or cannot attend for a legally justified reason. Its members include six justices. It deals with:

1- Resolving disputes involving contradiction between two irrevocable judgments passed on one subject if one or more of the litigants was a party to the judgments in conflict. In these cases, the Commission is obligated to rule in favor of one of the two sentences and will order that it be implemented to the exclusion of the other;

2- Resolving disputes between two courts over which of them has jurisdiction in a case.

3- What the Court Chief Justice refers to it of judgments and resolutions are within the Court jurisdiction in terms of the law by which these judgments and resolutions were passed specifically as related to civil cases and personal status cases.

3: Expanded Criminal Commission

Its formation and hearings are similar to those of the Expanded Civil Commission. The Expanded Criminal Commission covers:

1- Issues referred to the commission by the Chief Justice;

2- Resolving disputes between two criminal courts over which of them has jurisdiction in a case.

4: Civil Commissions (Technical Commissions)

Appellate Commission/Real Estate

This technical commission is chaired by a Deputy Chief Justice with at least four other justices sitting as members. It deals with:

1- Reviewing judgments and resolutions of Appellate Courts made on real estate cases under their original jurisdiction.

2- The Commission also deals with challenges from lawyers on their penalties and other matters under which the Lawyers Law No 173 of 1965 allows challenge to the.Civil Commission / Real Estate. In these cases the commission is presided over by a Deputy Chief Justice or a senior Commission member with membership of at least two other judges. It deals with challenges to judgments and resolutions on real estate and what branches off it to which no appeal challenges are lodged or which are not subject to appeal.

3- This commission can also review resolutions passed by the Oil Compensation Committee formed by Resolution No 1018 of 1982.

Appellate Commission / Chattels

This commission is presided over by a Deputy Chief Justice with membership of at least four other judges. The commission deals with:

1- The review of judgments and resolutions passed by Appellate Courts in their original capacity in matters related to chattels cases.

2- Addresses legal challenges submitted by the Chief Public Prosecutor in the public interest as stipulated by provisions of Article (30) of Public Prosecution Law No (159) of 1979.

Civil Commission / Miscellaneous Matters

This commission is also formed under a Deputy Chief Justice. It is used to address maters that do not clearly fall within the subject matter of other commissions, and is specifically used to review challenges to decisions of the Committee on the Retirees' Affairs in terms of the Third Clause of Article 20 of the Unified Retirement Law No. 27 of 2006 (amended by Law No. 69 of 2007).

5:   Personal Status Commissions

The First Personal Status Commission

This commission is presided by a Deputy Chief Justice or a senior Commission member with membership of at least two other judges. It deals with challenges to judgments and resolutions passed by Personal Status Courts according to their jurisdiction specified by Article (30) of the Amended Civil Procedure Law No 83 of 1969. It also looks into personal status issues of Non-Muslims.

Second Personal Status Commission

Its formation and hearings are similar to those of the First Commission. This commission is primarily concerned with challenges to judgments and resolutions on missing people and minors according to the Amended Care of Minors Law No. 78 of 1980.

6:   Criminal Commissions

First and Second Criminal Commissions

This two commission are each presided over by a Deputy Chief Justice or a senior Commission member and each then has at least four other Court judges. These commissions are concerned with challenges to judgments and resolutions passed by Criminal Courts (cases are divided between them).

Juvenile Commission

This commission is presided over by a Deputy Chief Justice or a senior Commission member with membership of at least two other judges. The commission deals with challenges to judgments and measures taken by the Juvenile Courts according to the Juvenile Delinquent Care Law No 76 of 1982.

7:   Reference Identification Commission

This commission is composed of six members, three of whom are selected by the Chief Justice from amongst Cassation Court members and three of whom are selected by the President of State from the Consultative Council. It is presided by the Chief Justice of the Court of Cassation according to Article Fourth/7 of the Amended State Consultative Council Law No. 69 of 1969. This commission reviews conflicts over jurisdiction between the Administrative Law Court and First Instance Courts. The commission's decision is final and binding on all parties.

The Court of Cassation has been at the center of disputes across civil and criminal areas since its formation, and has often had to navigate very difficult, and dangerous, political waters without the basic protections for the personal and professional safety of members discussed in earlier sections. In 1993, the Court received a major shock when ten of its members were placed on the retired list because of a judgment that the regime in power did not like. The decision to retire the ten justices caused widespread discontent among judicial and court staff, however since the executive maintained control over these types of actions there was little that could be done in response. The executive action had an impact on the independence of judicial decisions and judgments of the time.

After the downfall of the regime in 2003, there was a strong call in the judicial community that these judges be reinstated. Thanks to the earnest efforts made by many quarters, the Coalition Forces issued Order No (15), repealing the Resolution of 10 February, 1993 which placed the ten justices on the retired list. Justices Hishm Haj Ibrahim, Mudtafa al-Madamgha, Kreem Shareef, Ahmed al-Jaleeli, Hamid Sabha, Hishm Ahmed Deyaa, Farouk al-Sami and Muhammed Hassan Kashkul were reinstated and compensated accordingly, however a decade of service to the people of Iraq from ten talented and experienced judges had been lost. At the meeting that formally implemented the reinstatement of the judges in August, 2003, Justice Madhat al-Mahmood, who was in head of the Ministry of Justice at the time, gave the following speech:

> In the name of God, Most Gracious, Most Merciful
>
> We tell you their news rightly. They were young men who believed in their God and we supported their inspiration. We gave them courage when they stood up and said "O! God You are the God of Heaven and the Earth. We shall not call anyone by this name other than you." Allah says the truth.
>
> My Colleagues,
>
> It is a happy moment to see the dawn of the right rise over that which was wrong, making the latter dissipate — this is the day when our brothers from the Court of Cassation again take up their posts to speak the word of

truth, administer justice, and inspire confidence in the hearts of people who yearn for the day when stability, security and the rule of law prevail and when judicial independence supports a state based on law.

My heartfelt welcome is extended to my colleagues on their return to their posts. They gave us all a good example of standing by the right regardless of personal cost. Kind recognition is due to anyone who helped return our brothers to office; their return is a clear example of the resilience of the judiciary. With their return, we are united in our effort to build an independent judiciary seeking justice and righteousness for this country.

The table below shows the number of lawsuits resolved by the Federal Cassation Court:

Year	Civil Cases	Criminal Cases
2003	4929	1338
2004	30348	4128
2005	33330	6217
2006	17987	6492
2007	14167	9765
2008	15389	7823
2009	16351	10272
2010	19402	16138

Section C. Other Federal Courts Supported Through the Higher Judicial Council

Civil Courts

1- Appellate Courts

As discussed previously, Iraq has been divided into appellate districts since Ottoman times. While current districts are very similar to historic divisions, they are formally based on the structures established under the 2005 constitution, which differentiated between provinces that were part of a region and those that were not part of a regional structure. In 2005 only 3 provinces were combined to form the Kurdistan Region of Iraq. The areas outside of the Kurdistan Region are divided into sixteen judicial areas.[122]

Each appellate district is run by the Chief Justice of the appellate court for that district. The appellate court consists of the Chief Justice, his deputies and a number of judges whose number depends on the need. The Court exercises its jurisdiction as specified by law; Iraq is a civil law country so this is narrowly defined. All courts within the geographical jurisdiction of the appellate court are within the management responsibility of that appellate court.

---

[122] Baghdad Appellate Court- Al-Rusafa; Baghdad Appellate Court— Al-Karkh; Ninawa Appellate Court; Babel Appellate Court; Di Kaar Appellate Court; Kirkuk Appellate Court; Wassit Appellate Court; Diyala Appellate Court; Salahdin Appellate Court; Najaf Appellate Court; Anbar Appellate Court; Mayssan Appellate Court; Al-Muthana Appellate Court; Karbala Appellate Court; Kaadissiya Appellate Court; Baghdad Central Appellate Court

The Chief Justice of the Appellate Court distributes work among the judges and makes sure that sufficient number of staff and material supplies are provided to the courts from a shared budget allotted to that appellate district. If budgets are constrained by legislative or executive action, the budget allocated to each district will be limited based on an analysis of case loads, complexity and other factors. The Chief Justice of that appellate district then has the very difficult job of actively managing expenditures for all of the sub-courts within the district for the year based on lower-than-expected budget allocations.

The jurisdiction of an Appellate Court is as specified in Article 34 of the Civil Procedure Law:

1. To hear appeals from Courts of First Instance in the appellate district for lawsuits whose value does not exceed one thousand dinars;

2. To hear appeals on matters related to bankruptcy, company liquidation, and other matters which laws direct to the appellate court as a second-stage adjudication court;

3. Hearing appeals against judgments and resolutions from cases heard by first instance courts within the appellate district. For these cases, the appellate court is an investigating court and can review evidence, interview witnesses, etc. Cases may include:

    • Reviewing appeals of summary judgments and judgments passed based on claims that the judgments were based on evidence not on trial and other cases specified by Article 216/1 of the Civil Procedure Law;

• Other judgments and resolutions that specific laws state fall within the jurisdiction of the Appellate Court.

2- Courts of First Instance:

Article 21/1 of the Judicial Organization Law stated that "[o]ne or more First Instance Courts shall be set up in the center of each province or *qadaa* and can be set up in Nahiyya . . ." One judge is assigned to sit in each court of first instance. The Civil Procedure Law defines the jurisdiction of a court of first instance as follows:

1. Hearing civil lawsuits designated by Article 31 of the Civil Procedure Law. Its judgment is considered final, but can be appealed to the district's Appellate Court;

2. Hearing civil lawsuits designated by Article 32 of the Civil Procedure Law. Its judgment is considered final, but it can be appealed to the district's Appellate Court if the value of the case exceeds one thousand dinars;

3. Hearing civil lawsuits which require summary judgment as a matter of urgency to avoid injustice to a party.

3- Personal Status Court (For Non-Muslims):

The First Instance Court is the source of justice in matters of personal status for Non-Muslims in Iraq and for non-Iraqi Muslims from countries that do not apply Islamic Code to personal matters. Sentences in these cases are considered final, but they are subject to legal challenge at the Federal Cassation Court.[123]

4- Personal Status Court

Article 26 of the Judicial Organization Law states "[o]ne or more Personal Status Courts shall be set up wherever First Instance Courts exist . . ."

One Judge sits in a Personal Status Court. It deals with issues related to "personal status" as defined under Articles 300, 302 and 305 of the Civil Procedure Law. These include matters such as marital property and paternity, but they are not exclusive to other matters also being included. This court applies the provisions of the Personal Status Law No. 188 of 1959 to all individuals *except* those excluded by a special law, such as non-Muslims, that is applied to them. Its judgments are considered final, but are subject to appeal at the Federal Cassation Court.

5- Labor Court

Article 137 of Labor Law No. 71 of 1987 stipulated the establishment of one or more Labor Courts "in every province". One judge is assigned to sit in a Labor Court. Where there are not enough cases or resources to allow a dedicated court to be formed in a province, its jurisdiction is assigned to the Court of First Instance responsible for that province. A Labor Court looks into civil and criminal cases, as well as other disputes, relating to labor as stipulated in Labor Law, Laborers Retirement and Social Security Law and other legislation regarding employment, workplace conditions, or other matters related to labor.

---

[123] Madhat al-Mahmood, *Explanation of Civil Procedure Law*, 61.

The judgments of the labor court are considered final, but they are subject to appeal to the Federal Cassation Court.

Criminal Courts

1- Criminal Courts

The Higher Judicial Council establishes one or more criminal courts within each province. Each court must be chaired by the Chief Justice of the Appellate Court responsible for that province or one of his deputies with the additional membership of two judges. Criminal Courts look into criminal cases referred by an investigating court or misdemeanor court when the alleged crime is found to be outside of their jurisdiction. The criminal courts' judgments are deemed final, but are subject to appeal to the Federal Cassation Court.

Just as some cases are referred to the criminal courts by courts of first instance or misdemeanor courts, the criminal court itself may refer certain cases to other specialized criminal courts. For example, the Iraqi Central Criminal Court was formed by Order No. 12 of 2003 to investigate and prosecute serious criminal cases including terrorism cases. The Central Criminal Court uses many of the same procedural systems of other courts, however there are some unique aspects to the court. The Central Criminal Courts' judgments are also considered final, subject to appeal to the Federal Cassation Court.

The Central Criminal Court is composed of two courts:

1- Criminal Court, which consists of specialized commissions following the model of the Cassation Court;

2- Investigating Court, which processes most of the incoming cases and manages many of the linkages with law enforcement units and partners.

2- Misdemeanor Courts

A misdemeanor court is formed wherever a first instance court exists. One judge is typically assigned to the court, however should there not be enough cases or resources to allow one judge to be dedicated to the court, the first instance court judge will also be assigned responsibility for the misdemeanor court. The misdemeanor court, logically, specializes in misdemeanor cases that are referred to it by the investigating court. It adjudicates according to law and its judgments are deemed final, but subject to appeal to the appellate court responsible for the district in which it sits.

There are some specialized misdemeanor courts for matters such as traffic cases to manage areas where high caseloads are expected.

3- Juvenile Courts

A. Juvenile Delinquency Investigating Courts

These courts investigate crimes allegedly perpetrated by juveniles. Article 3 of the Juvenile Care Law No. 76 of 1983 defines a "juvenile" as someone that has attained the age of nine but has not reached the age of nineteen.

Only one judge sits in a Juvenile Delinquency Investigating Court, however there may be a number of judicial investigators and other supporting staff as caseloads require and resources allow. The judgments of this court are subject to appeal to the Juvenile

Delinquency Court in that court's capacity as a special Criminal Court for trying juveniles.

B. Juvenile Delinquency Court

This court addresses cases that involve a juvenile that is alleged to have committed a crime. It is chaired by a judge with membership of two additional jurors who are specialized in criminology or in a field related to juvenile matters. If the alleged offence is a misdemeanor, the judge alone will sit in the court.

Judgments passed by Juvenile Delinquency Court are considered final. If the case in question was civil in nature, then judgments may be appealed to the Federal Cassation Court. If the case in question was criminal, then the judgment must be appealed to the Federal Cassation Court regardless of whether involved parties request the appeal in accordance with Article 16 of the Public Prosecution Law No. 159 of 1979.

4- Customs Courts

Customs courts address cases relating to the assessment and collection of customs or duties. The court is chaired by a judge, who is joined by another judge and a director general. The director general must also be a law graduate. The two judges must both be of at least the second grade, and are nominated by the Higher Judicial Council. The director general is nominated by the Minister of Finance.

Custom court judgments are considered final, but are subject to appeal to the Cassation Commission formed according to Article 250 of the Customs Law No. 23 of 1984.

5- Investigating Courts

Article 35 of the Judicial Organization Law stipulated the formation of one or more investigating courts in every area where a court of first instance exists. One judge sits in each of these courts with a mandate to investigate all crimes.

The Judicial Organization Law permits the formation of specialized investigating courts. To date, Iraq has established several ad hoc and enduring specialized courts, including the Central Criminal Court of Iraq for complicated major crimes.

Section D. Courts Not Supported Through the Higher Judicial Council

In addition to the courts subordinate to Higher Judicial Council, there are other civilian courts which are not under the control of Higher Judicial Council, such as the Administrative Court managed by the State Consultative Council. As described below, these courts have judicial functions, yet they were overlooked during the rush to complete the major governance overhaul envisioned in 2003-2005 in preparation for the new constitution and remain under heavy executive control. In practice, these two courts constitute a violation of the concept of "judicial unity", and leave both the executive and judicial branches in an unfortunate position with regards to balancing constitutional mandates. As the middle class grows and economic opportunities blossom, the need for an independent resource for addressing claims against state bodies will clearly expand rapidly. Both the Administrative Court and the General Disciplinary Council should therefore be under the management of the Higher Judicial Council. Further, the decisions of the General Disciplinary Council should be linked to an appellate process within a competent judicial body as a matter of urgency.

1- Administrative Court

The Administrative Court addresses claims regarding administrative orders and decisions passed by government officials and government entities. This court was set up by Law No. 106 of 1989 and consists of a first-rank judge as a chair and two judges or assistant advisors from the State Consultative Council as members. Its judgments are subject to legal challenge at the Federal Supreme Court, and there are also appellate routes to the Federal Cassation Court for certain types of claims. The court has had its quarters in Baghdad since the issuance of the above-mentioned law in 1989.

2- General Disciplinary Council

The General Disciplinary Council is also beholden to State Consultative Council. This body provides a venue for government officials to appeal decisions made against them by their superiors. The General Disciplinary Council holds its sessions under chairmanship of the President of State Consultative Council, one of his deputies, or one of the judges on loan to the State Consultative Council. An additional two members are drawn from either the State Consultative Council or from judges on loan to the State Consultative Council. Its judgments are subject to appeal to the General Assembly of the State Consultative Council.

3- Courts of Provinces Legally Joined Into Regions, i.e. the Kurdistan Region

By operation of the Constitution, provinces that formally join together as regions have specific obligations and rights. The courts within regions are intended to be established independently from the federal courts. Currently only 3 provinces in the north of Iraq have formally established themselves as a region. This is of course the Kurdistan Region. However, the path is legally established for other provinces to join into regions so it is important to consider this arrangement more broadly. The people of the Kurdistan Region opted to establish a Kurdistan Judicial Council (KJC) in 2008 that operates to manage the courts in the Kurdistan Region in a manner similar to the Higher Judicial Council in Baghdad. The courts in the region receive all funding from their regional government. The 2005 Constitution was unfortunately silent on the formal relationship between the federal and regional courts, however the HJC and KJC have established healthy collegial relationships while waiting for constitutional and legal linkages to be clarified.

CHAPTER ELEVEN

Judicial Bodies Managed Within the Higher Judicial Council

Section A. The Public Prosecution

Some jurists define public prosecution within a civil-law system as a special kind judiciary representing the society. It should be mentioned that there are clay tablets establishing that the people of Iraq knew some aspects of the office of a public prosecutor since 2500 B.C. But other aspects of the modern office of a Public Prosecutor did not arrive until the 19th Century or later. During the Ottoman occupation, Iraq knew a very simple form of public prosecution. In 1879, the Ottoman government passed the Principles of Ottoman Criminal Procedure Law, which was itself adopted from the French law. This law described a civil-law public prosecution system for the entire Ottoman Empire, which at the time included the area of modern Iraq. Consistent with this law, the positions of public prosecutor and judicial investigator were started at that time.

This system continued until the British occupation of Basra in 1914-15 and the Law of Iraqi Occupied Areas was implemented. As discussed above, this law was extended to Baghdad after its occupation in 1917. The Baghdad Criminal Procedure Law (BCPL) came into force in December 1919 to replace the Ottoman Criminal Procedure Law. The Baghdad Criminal Procedure Law gave the public prosecutor different jurisdictions from those given under the Ottoman law. For example, the Baghdad Criminal Procedure Law empowered the public prosecutor to investigate crimes, question witnesses, and interrogate suspects in addition to the oversight authorities given in the Ottoman Criminal Procedure Law. The BCPL also gave the public prosecutor the authority to track the suspect and charge them. In short, the British law combined several roles and allowed the prosecutor to be both an investigator and a public prosecutor. However, it is important to note that the BCPL did not *mandate* that these roles be performed by a prosecutor: it permits bypassing the public prosecutor and allowed others to investigate or perform other functions in a prosecutions.

We can say that the BCPL combined two powers, the power to file a formal charge in a case and the power of investigation. Practically, however, it turned out that these two functions were often carried out by police at the time given the heavy British influence that remained. In 1925, the Minister of Justice abolished the job of public attorney[124] and transferred the position's roles formally to police actors. While practical under a British-inspired system, this executive decision created a number of complications within the largely civil-law system that remained in place in Iraq. On the recommendation of the Police Director General, the Minister of Justice named the Police Chief as the "investigating officer" and the Assistant Police Chief as the "assistant investigating officer." As a result of this ministerial action, police were authorized to follow up cases, attend hearings and submit legal challenges directly. Judges, who were also under the management of the Minister of Justice, were aligned to work under the supervision of the police.

However, in 1926 the Minister of Justice restored the job of public attorney under the now current title of "public prosecutor" suggesting that more professional education and experience was needed to manage criminal prosecutions than was available within the police.

---

[124] Translator's note: not clear at time of translation whether this "public attorney" role was defined in the BCPL as distinct from the "public prosecutor" role.

A public prosecutor was appointed in Basra, Hillah, and Diyalla provinces as well as in Baghdad. Public prosecutors were tasked with managing criminal cases and to provide advice when asked. When a public prosecutor was not available for a hearing, a police officer could stand in for them.

In 1931 the Appendix to the Baghdad Criminal Procedure Law No. 42 of 1931 (1931 Appendix) stipulated that the Minister of Justice needed to establish a Public Prosecution Office headed by a Chief Public Prosecutor. The Appendix further empowered the Minister to appoint public prosecutors when the need arose, while mandating that police officers would act as public prosecutors in areas where there was no public prosecutor. In a return to the civil-law tradition, the new Appendix also required the public prosecutors to defend the public interest on behalf of the government in criminal cases in accordance with separate regulations. The 1931 Appendix provided a foundation for rebuilding the public prosecution in Iraq following the experiments with British-style police prosecutions starting in 1925, however even with subsequent amendments the public prosecutors at the time felt that the laws fell short of those establishing prosecutorial offices in other advanced countries. Therefore, the 1925 BCPL, 1931 Appendix, and subsequent revisions had little long-term impact on the quality of justice in the country.

Since the job of a public attorney was abolished, its function was transferred to public prosecutors and the post of investigator was set up. The power to carry out investigation was lodged with police officers and law-graduates working at the Ministry of Justice under the direction of a judge. According to Article Six of the 1931 Appendix, a Public Prosecution Office headed by the Chief Public Prosecutor was established within the Ministry of Justice. The First Clause of Article Six formally replaced the designation "public attorney" with the term "investigator". Thus, by 1931 the power of public attorneys to investigate was transferred to investigators, who were mostly police officers, while the power to charge and manage the prosecution of criminal cases was lodged with the Chief Public Prosecutor and Public Prosecutors.

In 1932, a new Appendix to the Baghdadi Criminal Procedure[125] (1932 Appendix) further clarified and expanded the responsibilities of the Chief Public Prosecutor and other Public Prosecutors. Article Five of the 1932 Appendix law positioned the Chief Public Prosecutor and Public Prosecutors to oversee the work of investigators, including confirmation that investigators must follow the orders and instructions of designated prosecutors. This system remained largely intact for the next 4 decades.

In 1971, Criminal Procedure Law No. 65 of 1971 was passed. This law again refined the responsibilities of the Public Prosecution. In 1979, a law dedicated to the office, the Public Prosecution Law No. 159 of 1979, was issued. This law defined the Public Prosecution as consisting of the Chief Public Prosecutor, two Deputy Chief Public Prosecutors, and a number of Public Prosecutors and their deputies. The headquarters of Public Prosecution was confirmed to be in Baghdad, and the Public Prosecution was given national jurisdiction. While the 1979 law maintained the Public Prosecutors obligations with regard to filing cases in the public interest, managing criminal investigations, and giving advice when requested, the law also created the obligation for Public Prosecutors to challenge sentences and decisions passed by criminal courts, *Sulih* courts, and investigative courts. These last "oversight" obligations brought Iraq further back in line with civil law traditions. Public Prosecutors were also authorized to take over investigations when an investigative judge was absent and obligated to attend personal status hearings and cases. The shape of the Public Prosecutor position has remained intact since 1979.

In 2006, all Public Prosecutors were formally declared to be part of the judiciary in order to resolve confusion caused by the separation

---

[125]   Appendix to the Baghdad Criminal Procedure Law, No. 65 of 1932.

of the judiciary from the executive in preceding years.[126] This meant that the Higher Judicial Council could now assign Public Prosecutors as judges in criminal, misdemeanor, or investigative courts. The 2006 Appendix also confirmed that Public Prosecutors are subject to the same requirements as other judges, and are entitled to the same allowances, benefits, financial increases and promotion constraints as those applied to any other judge. Current levels of pay and benefits are discussed below.

The role of a Public Prosecutor has evolved from representing the public interest through advocacy and management of criminal investigations and prosecutions to one of also promoting the correct operation of the law within a constitutional framework. In light of the Public Prosecutor's ability to challenge judgments or intervene in investigations, the role is an essential check on both executive and judicial actors. The position ensures that the public interest is always represented in both criminal and personal status cases.

As discussed above, Article 89 of the Constitution of Iraq included the Public Prosecution as part of the federal judiciary along with the Higher Judicial Council, the Federal Supreme Court, the Federal Court of Cassation, and other federal courts. The 2006 Addendum to the Public Prosecution law resolves confusion over the placement of the Office of the Public Prosecutor by aligning the administration and management with the 2005 Constitution. Public Prosecutors are nominated by Higher Judicial Council to the parliament, which approves the appointment as specified by Article 91 of the 2005 Constitution.

Due to several decades of intense executive interference under the old regime, few in modern are fully aware of the role of the Office of Public Prosecution. In truth, many of the modern functions evolved from experience in civil law systems since the Ottomans

---

[126] Appendix to the Public Prosecutors Law of 1979, Law No. 10 of 2006.

brought French systems to Iraq in the 19th Century. The British modified some of these systems temporarily to align Iraqi with their police-centric investigation model, however subsequent efforts have resulted in a system that can be largely compared to the modern French structures at most levels. If we accept the linkage to the French system, then we can say that the origin of the modern Office of the Public Prosecution in Iraq dates back to the fourteenth century efforts in France. By 1971, the Public Prosecution had taken on an active role in guarding the public interest and emerging as an attorney acting on society's behalf.

The Office of the Public Prosecution now sits within the HJC, but it has maintained the structures established under previous laws to manage its affairs independently from the rest of the judiciary. Within the Office there is a Presidency of the Public Prosecution System, which consists of the President of the System as well as two deputies. The office of the Presidency is responsible for running the national efforts of the Public Prosecution administratively and technically.

Other technical committees within the Office of the Public Prosecution review criminal and juvenile delinquency cases that are subject to challenge either automatically or purposefully according to Article 16, Parts 1-2 of the Public Prosecution Law. These cases are forwarded from criminal and juvenile courts or filed directly by appellants or prosecutors operating from court districts. The technical committees within the Office of the Public Prosecution review the cases, draft legal opinions on the sentences passed or other issues raised, and then forward the cases to the Federal Cassation Court. In addition, the Office of the Public Prosecution includes the Committee for Challenge in the Benefit of the Law. This committee looks into sentences and judgments that are subject to legal challenge, but which have not been formally challenged by parties to the case. The cases must have the state, a minor or a ward of the state as a party, involve irregularity to public order, or cause harm to state property in order to qualify for review. These cases demonstrate most clearly how the Office of the Public Prosecution can operate in the public interest as the law allows the Office to challenge cases and judgments in the interest of society even if parties to the case are satisfied with the individual outcome.

The Iraqi public prosecution system shares some features with other Middle Eastern countries influenced by the Ottomans, yet its modern development has provided a unique environment that has allowed the Iraqi office to develop elements admired amongst regional partners in spite of significant challenges. Several critical contributions have also inspired the respect of the Iraqi public. The Public Prosecution now enjoys the same status as the rest of the Iraqi judiciary, and is a key partner in defending justice and building the state of law.

The Office of Public Prosecution is also well positioned as an autonomous oversight element within the HJC to monitor data related to crimes and cases within the court system, in fighting corruption within the courts, and in reviewing the potential need for, or impact of, new legislation or regulations. In recent years, the Office has initiated a survey of the types of crimes being addressed by the courts nationally along with analysis on how the HJC and government can best look after the public interest in light of the changing face of crime. Some of the Office's analysis is generated to evaluate legislation in light of the current legal environment and criminal trends. Moreover, the Office of Public Prosecution plays a major role in fighting the corruption that remains widespread in government bodies following the fall of the former regime, which was rife with social diseases that continue to threaten the rule of law.

One of the techniques used by the old regime to control judges and oversight bodies such as the Office of the Public Prosecution was to severely constrain the pay and benefits of the professional staff. This technique left judges and public prosecutors heavily dependent on the largesse of political leaders for fees or pay related to membership on special government bodies, scholarships for their children, or support for travel and professional development. The public prosecutors were particularly aggrieved between 1988 and 2003 as they were passed over when judges received a pay increase in 1988. As an example, a first grade judge's salary before April 9th 2003 was Iraqi Dinar (IQD) 774 thousand while, on the other hand, a first grade public prosecutor's pay was IQD 129 thousand.[127] The injustice of this and the fact that the disparity was related to efforts of tyrannical control by the old regime led the HJC to advocate with the US Administrator for Iraq for standardizing judicial and prosecutor pay soon as soon as possible after the HJC's formation. Subsequently, the HJC advocated for unifying the judicial and prosecutor designations in Law No. 10 of 2006.[128] In later years, the HJC has been able to successfully advocate for increases to judicial (including prosecutor's) salaries, which now sit at:

- Fourth grade judge: IQD 1,000,000,

- Third grade judge or prosecutor: IQD1 ,250,0000,

- Second grade judge or prosecutor: IQD 1,500,000,

- First grade judge or prosecutor: IQD 1,750,000.

During the first decade of 2000, judges and prosecutors faced increasing threats of violence against themselves and their families. In response, the HJC requested a risk allowance from the Council of Ministers. Consequently, the Council of Ministers in session thirty five of 2005 granted judges (including public prosecutors) a risk allowance equaling 50% of their salaries. In 2007, the Council

---

[127] Editor's Note: In January 2014, the Iraqi Dinar was worth USD .0008598, so IQD 129,000 = approximately USD 110.90.

[128] Law No. 10 of 2006, Amendment to the Law to General Prosecution Law No. 159 of 1979, Article (1), which states: "[p]ublic prosecutors who are still in service shall be regarded as judges consistent with their grade, class, seniority and position they are in at the time this Law is issued. The provisions which are applied to judges shall be applied to them. They shall also enjoy the rights and privileges of judges."

of Ministers agreed agreed to increase this allowance to 100% of the salaries as violence continued to escalate and judges and prosecutors were forced to fund their own security. Thus the salaries of judges, public prosecutors have become as follows:

- Fourth grade judge: IQD 2,000,000,

- Third grade judge or prosecutor: IQD 2,500,000,

- Second grade judge or prosecutor: IQD 3,000,0000,

- First grade judge or prosecutor: IQD 3,500,000.

In 2008 base salaries were finally increased.[129] This was the first increase in base salaries for judges since 1998. Risk allowances were also increased to 150% and new job allowances were introduced on top of the new base salary rates. The new base salary rates were now:

- Fourth grade judge: IQD 1,500,000,

- Third grade judge or prosecutor: IQD 1,750,0000,

- Second grade judge or prosecutor: IQD 2,000,000,

- First grade judge or prosecutor: IQD 2,500,000.

Thus, in 2008 the total remuneration of judges and public prosecutors including basic salary, job allowance and risk allowance was raised to:

- Fourth grade judge: IQD 4,500,000,

- Third grade judge or prosecutor: IQD 5,250,0000,

---

[129]   Law No. 27 of 2008.

- Second grade judge or prosecutor: IQD 6,000,000,

- First grade judge or prosecutor: IQD 6,750,000.

Consistent with the independence of Iraqi judiciary, the Higher Judicial Council is currently working on developing principles and guidelines on the operation of the Office of Public Prosecution to draw additional benefits from the experience and skills of the prosecutors.

Over the history of independent Iraq several prominent legal figures took over the presidency of Office of Public Prosecution, including the judge and legal scholar Professor Abdul Ameer al-Ukaili, who was president of Public Prosecution in 1959, and a number of judges from the Federal Cassation Court. Cassation Court members assigned to the Presidency included Judges Salim Ubayd al-Umaan, Abdul Jabbar Dalla Ali, Malik al-Hindawi, Ghassan Jameel al-Wiswassi, Adnan Abdul Razzak, Ayadd Abdul Hameed, Tarik Naji, Kassim Ridha Alu, Nashaat Hassan Taha, and, finally, Gudanfir Hamoud al-Jassim who took over in April, 2003. Judge Gudanfir started first as Deputy Chief Public Prosecutor and then Chief Public Prosecutor before becoming President.

Section B. Judicial (Justice) Oversight Commission

History of the Judicial Oversight Commission

Article 22, Clause 1 of the Courts Formation Declaration of 28 November 1917 mandated the Minister of Justice to supervise all civil and civil status courts and the Federal Cassation Court to manage all subordinate bodies thereof, being guided by the authority of the Minister. Under this system, the Federal Cassation Court received performance data from all courts nationally on request. The Court then submitted data and management recommendations to the Minister of Justice.

Several sets of regulations were promulgated guide the review of the justice sector generally before any specific guidance was passed to directly structure the review of the judiciary itself. In 1930, the Office for the Inspection of Justice Affairs was created by the Minister of Justice through Judicial Regulations No. 1 of 1948. The Minister also set up the Inspection Committee within the Ministry of Justice, consisting of three inspectors selected by the Minister out of first-rank judges or the top grade of the second-rank judges. For inspection purposes, Iraq was divided into four regions. In 1953, the Judicial Regulations No. 34 of 1953 gave instruction to investigators to review the number of cases filed, how many cases were resolved during a year, and reasons for cases to remain unresolved. Other provision of the regulations give guidance on how to inspect other institutions within the Ministry and how to resolve breeches of policy or law made by judges and officials.

Finally, in 1956 Judicial Service Law No. 58 was passed to regulate the judiciary in Iraq by establishing a Judicial Oversight Commission. This is a full eleven years after the judiciary took shape through the Judicial Service Law No. 27 of 1945. The Judicial Oversight Commission was set up to take over investigation into the actual performance of judges in managing their responsibilities as administrators and as judges. The most important innovation of this law was the re-establishment of the Judges and Qadis Committee under the name "Judges and Qadis Affairs Committee". Among its members were the President of Judicial Oversight Commission, the Deputy Chief Justice of the Federal Cassation Court, and a senior judge or a high-ranking official from the Ministry of Justice selected by the Minister selected at the beginning of each calendar year. The Chief Justice of the Court of Cassation continued to head the Committee. When looking into a Qadi-related issue, the Committee was joined by the Chairmen of the Councils of Cassation on Personal Status as members.

In 1960, Article 1 of the Judicial Investigation Law again stipulated the formation of the Judicial Oversight Commission in the Ministry of Justice. Under the 1960 law, the Commission was made up of a president and no less than nine investigators to carry out the duties stipulated in the law. The law moved dramatically towards executive dominated review of the judiciary. On August 18, 1967 the Judicial Investigation Law was replaced by the gazetting of the Judicial Oversight Commission Law No. 115 of 1966. Over the ensuing decade, experience demonstrated that a number of changes were needed to better support the evolution of the judiciary and support justice. These changes were incorporated into the Judicial Oversight Law No. 124 of 1979.

Following the 1979 law, there was a long period of legislative silence on the matter of judicial oversight. This silence closely coincided with the rise of the Bathist regime and its efforts to subjugate non-executive elements of the government. In light of the rebirth of judicial independence in 2003, as documented in the 2005 Constitution, the HJC endeavored to replace the 1979 law with a law that reflected the new judicial branch, the membership of the Judicial Oversight Commission as part of the Judicial Authority as stated in Article 89 of the 2005 Constitution, and changes in the Ministry of Justice to accommodate the Constitution. As an intermediate measure, the HJC restricted jobs within the Judicial Oversight Commission to judges and members of the public prosecution. Among the judges who worked in the new Judicial Oversight Commission were Abdul Fattah Mohammed Salim al-Urfali, Abdul Hussein al-Tae, Shawkit Babaan, Kamal Umer Nathmi, Rashid Ba-Jelaan, Abdul Jabaar al-Karaguli, Mohammed Zaynil, Sami Abdul Hameed, Abdul Kadir Taha, Sakin al-Unrachi, Khayre Ameen al-Shamma, Tarik Hassan Ul-Mamuri, Mustafa Kadhim al-Mudamgha, Hassan Aziz Abdul Rahman, Faruk Yassin al-Ammer, Faruk Hamuda, Abdul Karim al-Zehree, Ahmed al-Araji, Hussein Abu al-Temin, Najii Habaish, Abul Hussein Shandil, Kahttan al-Ugrareem and Saadi Sadik al-Ubaydee.

Justice supervisors who were not judges used to supervise Ministry of Justice institutions other than courts such as Real Estate Registration

Departments and Minor Property Departments. Among them Younis al-Muslih, Hamid al-Sakbaan, Abdul al-Azez al-Hassani, and Mohammed Bakir Ali. These officers were appointed according to Article 30 of the Judicial Oversight Commission Law, No. 115 of 1966, which authorized the appointment of non-judges to manage Ministry of Justice institutions other than courts and public prosecution offices. Managers appointed under this provision must be first grade officials of the Ministry of Justice, hold a first degree in law, have legal and administrative competence, and have no less than ten years of service in different departments of the Ministry of Justice. These officers could be appointed by presidential decree on the recommendation of the Minister.

The Work of the Judicial Oversight Commission

According to the Judicial (Justice) Oversight Commission Law, No. 124 of 1979,[130] the Commission consisted of a president, two deputy presidents, and justice supervisors and judges sufficient for performing duties. The Commission's headquarters were established in Baghdad, and its work was broadly defined as the inspection and supervision of the work of officials granted judicial authority. In practice, the Judicial Oversight Commission developed two lanes of operations to manage its obligations. First, a national inspection program was developed. Inspection programs require significant staff and travel budgets, so in the tight fiscal environment of the former regime these inspections were constrained. Secondly, the Commission

---

[130] Editor's Note: The Arabic word for justice and judge does not translate simply into English; the common practice is to call the body created by Law No. 124 of 1979 the "Judicial Oversight Commission", however in reality this body has a number of functions that cover actors that are not judges and institutions that are not staffed by judges. These obligations are discussed briefly later in this section. In light of this, the body is sometime referred to as the "Justice Oversight Commission". Rather than use two different names and imply that there are two different bodies, this edition will use the common "Judicial Oversight Commission" following this note.

established a mechanism for complaints to be submitted against judges or staff of institutions within the Commission's purview. Under Law No. 124 of 1979, the Commission reported to the Ministry of Justice. The Commission shifted to the HJC when that body was re-established in 2003.

Articles One and Two of the Judicial Oversight Commission Law state its objectives:

1. Ensure that courts and Ministry of Justice institutions carry out their duties involving the enforcement and respect for the laws;

2. Review the performance of judges and officials granted judicial authority in resolving disputes;

3. Assess blockages in the dispute resolution process and make appropriate recommendations to address them;

4. Follow up on the implementation of strategic plans for upgrading institutions related to dispute resolution and support staff and management in overcoming any problems;

5. Recognize outstanding personnel so that they can be nurtured and appropriately posted.

To achieve these objectives, the Judicial Oversight Commission Law directs the completion of the following activities for the Commission:

1. Guide and instruct judges and officials of the Ministry of Justice [now the HJC] institutions on the best way to perform their duties;

2. Supervise and evaluate performance by documenting faults and challenges with the delivery of justice along with potential solutions;

3. Assess how well officials are maintaining the property entrusted to them;

4. Evaluate the competency of justice institutions in doing their duties and recommend appropriate measures for improvement (if needed);

5. Hold seminars and workshops for officials to discuss findings, review options for improvements, and reduce obstacles.

By September 2003, the HJC had refined the obligations of the Judicial Oversight Commission around its legislative mandate. The core responsibilities of the Commission were the supervision of:

1. All courts "subordinate to the Ministry of Justice"[131] except the Cassation Court,

2. Public Prosecutors,

3. Ministry of Justice institutions other than Ministry headquarters and the State Consultative Council,

4. Officials granted judicial authority.

The shift of the Judicial Oversight Commission to the HJC in 2003 was further formalized under Part Six of the Law of Administration for the State of Iraq for the Transitional Period in 2004. In 2005, Article 89 of the Constitution of the Republic of Iraq formally included the Judicial Oversight Commission within the independent judicial branch of the new democratic system: "The Federal Judicial Authority shall be composed of the Higher Judicial Council, the

---

[131] Following the re-establishment of the Higher Judicial Council in 2003 courts formerly subordinate to the Ministry of Justice were shifted under the HJC with the few exceptions noted above.

Federal Supreme Court, the Federal Cassation Court, the Office of the Public Prosecution, the Judicial Oversight Commission and other Federal Courts."

Section C. General Administration of the Higher Judicial Council

1- Office of Judges and Public Prosecutors' Affairs

This office was set up by Cabinet order No. 134 of 13 November 2008 to manage operational matters relating to judges and public prosecutors such as promotion, retirement conditions, data relating to staffing, judicial administrative orders, court formation, and secretariat support for the HJC meetings. The Office consists of the Department of Personnel and the Department of Service Calculation (Retirement). The former prepares all necessary documents for the promotion of judges and public prosecutors and manages files on issues forwarded to the HJC for review. In the case of allegations of illegal or improper behavior, the Department of Personnel issues the orders referring individuals to the Disciplinary Committee when instructed by the HJC. The Department of Service Calculation (Retirement) issues orders regarding pensions and other entitlements on the retirement of judges and public prosecutors based on either the individual having reached the mandatory retirement age or on health grounds. This Department also manages final benefits and closes files when judges and prosecutors pass away. Along with developing improved systems for managing retirement and other benefits, the Department of Service Calculation also assumed responsibility for processing the administrative orders relating to leave, applications for service extension, and other retirement-related matters.

The Department of Personnel maintains complete files on judges and public prosecutors. The HJC has led the justice sector in digitizing records by creating a world-class IT Department that has established practical systems for the HJC's administrative units and supported the training of staff. The Department of Personnel established an Oracle-based database in which it manages all developments in the records of judges and public prosecutors based on the administrative orders issued by the Office of Judges and Public Prosecutors' Affairs or by a District Court. This database allows the Department to prepare reports and analyze statistics as requested. Key items tracked include staff numbers, staff classifications, court types and staffing, and the rank and position of staff within each court. As of 2012, the rough scope of the court services are demonstrated by the following sets of data. Some of the tables below are combined from a number of different reports and should be considered indicative given the complexity of the administrative systems in place. Official and current information should be sourced from the Department of Personnel.

Position	Number
Total Number of Judges	925
Total Number of Public Prosecutors	338
Number of Federal Supreme Court Judges	9
Female Judges (Total)	15
Female Prosecutors (Total)	52
Female Judges (in Baghdad Only)	10
Female Prosecutors (in Baghdad)	29
Number of First Grade Judges	152
Number of First Grade Prosecutors	56
Number of Second Grade Judges	186
Number of Second Grade Prosecutors	20
Number of Third Grade Judges	255
Number of Third Grade Prosecutors	71
Number of Fourth Grade Judges	304
Number of Fourth Grade Prosecutors	194
Newly Appointed Judges (2012)	2
Number of Martyred Judges (as of 2012)	47

	Court District / Assignment	Chief Justice of District	Deputy Chief Justice of District	Judges	Public Prosecutors	Investigative Judges
1	Al Rusafa	2	22	120	37	41
2	Al Karkh	3	10	56	15	29
3	Central/ Al Karkh	0	5	35	19	12
4	Ninevah	2	8	76	28	0
5	Al Basra	2	6	62	30	21
6	Babil	3	9	64	27	20
7	Al Najaf	2	4	36	12	13
8	Wassit	4	4	32	15	19
9	Al Anbar	1	12	46	14	17
10	Diyala	0	7	49	21	22
11	Kirkuk	3	8	52	13	10
12	Salah Al Din	3	8	49	20	14
13	Thi Qar	0	5	50	19	18
14	Al Muthana	4	4	31	9	9
15	Maysan	1	4	38	13	12
16	Al Qadisiyah	2	4	45	14	12
17	Karbala	1	6	35	16	12
18	Judicial Oversight	1	3	7	0	0
19	Public Prosecution Presidency	0	2	0	17	11[1]
20	Outside of Courts	0	2	9	1	0
21	Other Special Rank Judges	0	0	0	0	8
22	HJC Headquarters	0	0	1	0	0
23	Federal Cassation Court	0	0	28	0	11[2]
	Totals	34	133	921	340	311

1   Number extrapolated from other charts provided by the HJC.
2   Number extrapolated from other charts provided by the HJC.

113

Higher Judicial Council / List of Courts by Type (2010)

Name of Appellate Courts	Court of Appeal	Criminal	Juvenile	Labor	Trade	First Instance	Personal Affairs	Misdemeanor	Investigative	Customs	Mass Media	Total	Criminal Commissions
Federal Al Rusafa	1	1	1	1	1	10	9	10	11	1	1	46	4
Federal Al Karkh	1	1	1	-	-	6	7	4	8	-	-	28	1
Federal Ninawa	1	1	1	1	1	14	14	14	17	1	-	65	2
Federal Dyala	1	1	1	1	1	11	11	11	11	-	-	49	1
Federal Babil	1	1	1	1	1	13	13	13	13	-	-	57	2
Federal Al Najaf	1	1	1	1	1	7	7	7	7	-	-	33	1
Federal Kirkuk	1	1	1	1	1	7	7	7	8	-	-	34	2
Federal Thi Qar	1	1	1	1	1	11	11	11	11	-	-	49	1
Federal Al Anbar	1	1	1	1	1	10	10	10	10	1	-	46	2
Federal Al Basra	1	1	1	1	1	10	10	10	17	1	-	53	2
Federal Wasit	1	1	1	1	1	9	9	9	9	-	-	41	1
Federal Salah iddin	1	1	1	1	1	12	12	12	13	-	-	54	1
Federal Al Muthana	1	1	1	1	1	4	4	4	4	-	-	21	1
Federal Misan	1	1	1	1	1	6	6	6	7	-	-	30	1
Federal Karbala	1	1	1	1	1	5	5	5	5	-	-	25	1
Federal Al Qadisiah	1	1	1	1	1	8	8	8	8	-	-	37	1
CCCI/ Al Karkh	-	1	-	-	-	-	-	-	1	-	-	2	2
Total	16	17	15	15	15	143	143	141	160	4	1	670	26

Rasafa	Karkh	Ninwa	Diyala	Najaf	Babil	Dhi Qar	Kirkuk	Anbar	Wasit	Salah Aldin	Muthana	Misan	Karbala	Basra	Diwaniya
Rasafa	Karkh	Musil	Ba'quba	Najaf	Hillah	Nasriyyah	Kirkuk	Ramadi	Kut	Tikrit	Samawah	Amarah	Karbal	Basrah	Diwaniyah
Adamiyyah	Baya	Shamal	Quraiba	Kufa	Suddah	Rifa'i	Huwaijah	Falujah	Swairah	Samira	Khadir	Majar Kabeer	Hindiyah	Ma'kal	Ghmas
Karadih	Kadimiya	TalAfar	Sadiyyah	Abassiyah	Mashro'	Suq Alshurokh	Daquq	Habaniyyah	Al-Hay	Balad	Rmaitha	Kahla	Husayniyah	Shat Alarab	Shamiyyah
Baghdad AlJadeedah	AbuGharib	Rabee'ah	Balad Rose	Haydariyyah	Qasim	Qala Sukar	Dibis	Karmah	Azizyyah	Dijail	Warka	Qal2at Sukar	Ain Tamir	Abi Khasib	Hamzah
Al-Thawrah	Mahmodiyah	Sinjar	Jalwla'	Manathirah	Mahaweel		Zab	Haditha	Nu'maniyyah	Toz	4	Maymuna	Har	Faw	Afak
Al-Zuhor	Tarmiyyah	Ba'aj	Khalis	Mishkhab	Musayyib	Jabayish	Riyad	Hiit	Zubaydiyyah	Sharqat		Ali AlGharbi	5	Zubair	Mihnawiyah
Al-Mada'in	6	Hadhar	AbiSaida	Qadissiyah	Iskandariyyah	Shatrah	Alton Kubri	Annah	Badrah	Beji		6		Safwan	Shnafryah
Al-Sha'ab		Hamam AlAkeel	BaniSa'd	7	Kafil	Islah	7	Rawah	Sheik Sa'ad	Dur				Madinah	Dagharah
8		Talkeef	Muqdadiyah		Madahiyyah	Batha'		Qa'im	Ahrar	Yathrib				Dair	8
		Hamdaniyah	Mandali		Hashmiyyah	Nasir		Ratbah	9	Dhlu'iyah				Qarnih	
		Shikhan	Mansoriyyah		Abu Gharaq	Gharaf		10		Ishaky				10	
		Makhmour	11		Shumaly	11				Al-Alam					
		Zamar			Taleea'h					12					
		Kiyarah			13										
		14													

115

2- **Office of Administrative Affairs and Judicial Security**

The HJC responded quickly to address the needs of courts. Judges, and staff by establishing dedicated administrative and security resources soon after its formation. Prior to 2003, all courts and staff were supported by the much larger, policy driven, engine of the Ministry of Justice. During times of limited budgets, courts and related services, such as training, were highly curtailed. In conjunction with other elements discussed above, the lack of administrative support resulted in a decline in the provision of services, especially to rural communities. The HJC committed itself to ensuring that judges, courts, and staff were appropriately resourced for the safe, effective delivery of services. These resources create the necessary foundation for judges to apply the law objectively and fairly. In response to the requirements of the renewed mandates and the independent status of the judiciary, the HJC increased the number of staff from 3156 at the time of its establishment in 2003 to 5630 employees by 2010. Some of these positions addressed needs that were formally supported through the Ministry of Justice, while other forged new capacity in areas such as IT. The HJC also established a specialized judicial and court security arm to address the vicious attacks on courts, judges and court staff. On separation from the Ministry of Justice, the HJC was left without any trained security staff positions or dedicated police support. Building from a cadre of contract staff, the HJC built a security arm of 5300 contractors and staff by 2012 to address the security needs of the judicial and administrative staff and citizens visiting courthouses.

The HJC organizational structure define the tasks of the Office of Administrative Affairs and Judicial Security as:

1. Analyzing the staffing needs for the administrative and security work force and fill positions with highly qualified and well trained staff;

2. Manage employee affairs within the HJC;

3. Manage judicial, staff, and court security at all HJC managed sites around the country;

4. Develop special training courses to qualify judicial investigators and improve employee efficiency based on critical work obligations;

5. Prepare plans to develop administrative activity and answer inquiries received from HJC administrative sub-offices;

6. Manage employees' promotions, salary increases, and service calculations according to the law;

7. Manage all correspondence with HJC sub-offices and relevant other offices;

8. Manage, issue, and follow up the administrative orders issued by the HJC or District Courts to ensure personnel records and related are up to date;

9. Develop software and other IT solutions for HJC offices that meet Government of Iraq standards and international best practices, supervise their installation and operation, and train employees on IT system use and maintenance;

10. Issue ID cards for HJC employees and control access to data and facilities;

11. Manage judicial security affairs, hire and train judicial and court guards, provide courts and staff with equipment and supplies, manage security operations;

12. Provide technical and operational services to the HJC headquarters and annexes of the HJC, and provide advanced technical guidance and support to District Courts that request assistance;

13. Provide secure, efficient transportation services to judges, public prosecution personnel and employees and maintain safe and well-kept HJC vehicles.

The Office of Administrative Affairs and Judicial Security is composed of the Employees' Affairs Department, Judicial Security, the Maintenance Department, the Social Research Committee, the Nursery, and the Computer / IT Department.

3- Office of Public Relationships and Legal Affairs

The Office of Public Relations and Legal Affairs was formed by Cabinet Order No. 133 of 2008 to:

1. Manage the relationship between offices within the HJC and between the HJC and other government actors;

2. Analyze issues and deliver legal opinions about matters as requested from the HJC;

3. Develop strategic plans and establish a comprehensive statistical and reporting system;

4. Represent the HJC before the courts when the HJC is a party to a case;

5. Review the implementation of strategic plans;

6. Create tools for linking the HJC, judicial, and court services to the public to improve citizen access to services and, ultimately, their rights.

The Office of Public Relations and Legal Affairs consists of the following departments:

- Public Relationships Department.

- Legal Affairs Department.

- Planning and Statistics Department.

- Social Research Commission

4- Office of Financial Affairs

This Office manages all of the fiduciary issues within the HJC and subsidiary bodies in strict compliance with the Financial Administration Law (FAL). The FAL stipulates the kind of expenditures that the Office of Financial Affairs is authorized to deal with, while the Federal Public Budget Law specifies the financial allocations that the Office of Financial Affairs is able to access for a given budget year. The HJC made financial compliance a priority since its formation, and each department within the HJC is required to establish and operate within an activity-based budget each year in line with Government of Iraq regulations. The Office of Financial Affairs prepares a monthly budget covering expenses and revenues incurred during the month. This technical budget is detailed and includes all account activity that can reflect on the financial status of the HJC. The budget shows the liquidity status of the institution, and produces a trial balance that shows the allocations received from the Ministry of Finance against approved budget lines and projected spending for the month using the allocations. As with any government budget, approved budgets are not all released at the beginning of the year, so the Office of Financial Affairs is tasked with presenting revenue streams and projected expenditures to the management of the HJC each month in order to adjust expenditures to align with resources on hand. The goal of the Office of Financial Affairs is to be accurate when using public money, to spend money only for the purpose it was allocated for, and, finally, to accurately report on financial items on the schedule dictated by appropriate authorities.

The tasks of this office include the following:

1. Prepare the financial plan for the HJC, accommodating all subsidiary spend units;

2. Organize the work of the financial and accounting departments, seeking to simplify procedures and modernize outputs;

3. Prepare reports on financial inquiries received by the Financial Department;

4. Manage the implementation of the financial plan developed by the HJC;

5. Dispense salaries and allowances as authorized by the relevant Offices;

6. Conduct transfers and additions for the judiciary according to the authority granted by the federal Budget Law;

7. Maintain the financial and accounting records stipulated in accounting regulations and laws and keep formal records;

8. Provide the general administration of the HJC and the relevant offices with stationary, furniture and other operational needs;

9. Provide cash flow (for both the regular and investment budget) by coordinating with relevant Government of Iraq institutions and the HJC leadership;

10. Supervise relationships and correspondence related to spending;

11. Audit the financial transactions (for both regular and investment budget) according to the generally accepted accounting fundamentals;

12. Directly pay the pensions for judges and public prosecutors as authorized by relevant Offices.

The office is formed from the following departments:

- Budgeting

- Expenses

- Salaries

- Follow-up

- Engineering

- Warehouse

- Retirement

- Contracts

- Auditing

- Post spending audit

- Cashier

- General Administration

5- Directorate General of the Legal, Administrative, and Financial Affairs in the Federal Supreme Court

A Cabinet Order in 2005 established the Directorate General of Legal, Administrative, and Financial Affairs. The Directorate is headed by a Director General and consists of three departments that manage the affairs of the Federal Supreme Court itself:

1. The Legal Affairs Department which deals with legal affairs including lawsuit management;

2. Human Resources Department which takes care of administrative affairs of court personnel;

3. Financial Affairs Department which runs the financial affairs of the court.

6- Mass Media Center of Higher Judicial Council

The HJC established the Mass Media Center to improve cooperation with Iraqi and international mass media in line with international practices that recognize the important role of the media in keeping citizens well connected to the institutions available for the resolution of disputes and protection of rights. The Mass Media Centre disseminates materials on legal and court matters, and is composed of two sections, Judicial Mass Media and Archiving and Research. The Center reports directly to the President of the HJC.

Since its establishment, the Mass Media Center (MMC) has developed lanes to both traditional print and electronic media outlets. The MMC has also delivered targeted programs to disseminate important legal information and raise awareness of the courts in society.

Since its establishment, the Mass Media Center has succeeded in overcoming many obstacles that journalists faced under the previous regime, which sought to hide many cases from the public. The MMC provides media outlets with the accurate and timely news updates, reports, and statistics regarding the activities of the Higher Judicial Council and subsidiary courts and institutions.

The MMC also seeks to ensure that the HJC is well briefed on media items that could impact on the HJC, courts generally, or cases before the courts. Because of the sensitivity, importance and preciseness of the operations of the Higher Judicial Council and related institutions, access to informations is a critical tool for the administration of justice. The Center provides this tool by following news bulletins, websites, social media, and daily newspapers for any relevant information. The MMC tabulates the informations and archives it for easy access as needed. The archive has become an information database for the Council.

7. Judicial Development Institute (JDI)

The Chief Justice Reviews the JDI with the
Director—2010

In early 2008, and with the assistance and support of the Department of State Bureau of International Narcotics and Law Enforcement (INL), work started on the creation of the Judicial Development Institute (JDI). The HJC developed the JDI in order to address critical gaps in staff capacity left by the years of executive neglect to the judiciary and courts under the old regime. As a new institution in a complicated environment, there were also many new demands on the staff of the HJC, related institutions, and courts. For example, the HJC needed to establish highly qualified security personnel and train court staff nationally on complicated new IT systems but it did not have the staff, resources, or venue to manage this obligation and no other government entity was providing sufficient access to their facilities. The HJC was also keen to advance the access of senior judges to information needed to manage new, complicated crimes involving terrorism, international commercial transactions, cyber-crime and other areas.

By far the most challenging aspect of establishing the institution was developing the leadership and administrative structures that could ensure judicial and staff investment in the development of curriculum, implementation of training programs, and operation of the institute. From the first, the HJC dedicated very senior and experienced judges and staff to lead this effort, and the Chief Justice personally invested in meetings with senior partners as the need arose. In addition to the administrative and operational systems built between 2008-2009, the HJC established a large compound of prefabricated structures. Due to financial and logistical limitation, this compound was constructed in stages according to judicial training requirements and portions will be upgraded to permanent structures as additional resources are available. Upon completion of core stages, the HJC issued order No. 929 / Office / 2009 of Sept 16, 2009 to formally establish the JDI. Further work continued to improve the compound through 2013.

The JDI functions have been supervised by a senior advisory committee, which was formalized in HJC Order No. 929, and managed by a senior administrator and dedicated staff. The Advisory Committee, sometime referenced as the Scientific Committee by English speaking partners, is mandated to:

1.   Supervise training activities at the JDI;

2. Establish curriculums by overseeing curriculum development processes that meet Iraqi and international best practices;

3. Select teaching staff;

4. Review recommendations for courses and events from judges, staff and international partners and propose professional judicial seminars;

5. Approve nominations of participants for courses;

6. Plan or approve professional courses, including their duration, criteria for participant selection, methodology and materials;

7. Suggest strategic development plans for the JDI to continue to expand its capacity to meet the HJC's needs;

8. Work with HJC leadership to assist Offices in developing strategic capacity development plans for staff, and with Courts to create capacity development plans for judiciary at specific ranks and within specific technical areas.

In 2008 the HJC launched the first survey of judges to document their perceived training needs. More than 80% of the judges responded in a very short time frame in spite of the significant security and logistical challenges present in Iraq at the time. This survey offered an early glimpse into the personal dedication of the judiciary to personal growth, and allowed the HJC to align the first phases of courses. Subsequent input was received from the administrative teams; early priorities included security awareness training, technical security skills for security personnel, statistics training on data collection, and the roll-out of the HJC's cases management system, which was the first Oracle system developed by an Iraqi justice institution. The JDI allowed the HJC's staff to fully develop the system and manage the roll-out of the system to regional staff with carefully timed training programs at the JDI's computer training lab. The JDI continues to pursue its goals of planning professional courses to upgrade the efficiency, capabilities and practical skills of judges and public prosecutors and other employees of the judiciary. During the time period from its establishment to mid-2011, the JDI held 43 courses and events in which 960 participants from the judiciary and executive bodies (including the police) took part. By 2013 approximately 3000 individuals had benefitted from courses at the JDI, and JDI management was targeting a schedule where courses and events supported by the HJC, other Iraqi institutions, or international partners would be hosted each week. Unfortunately, although the HJC began dedicating significant portions of the operational budget of the JDI starting in 2009, by 2013 political issues resulted in significant budget challenges that could restrict the further growth of the JDI if not resolved. See the Addendum to the Introduction of this book for more details.

8- Judicial Authority Website

HJC Order No. 143/M/2005 of August 2005 established a branch dedicated to providing the public with legal and court information. The branch, called the HJC Media Center, reports to the President of the HJC and has the narrowly constructed mandate to:

1. Capture all legal and court information electronically and organize it in by date and topic. The core information includes:

    a. All legal documents (laws, resolution which have the power of law, regulations, formal instructions)

    b. Resolutions and judgments of the Federal Cassation Court that set a precedent

    c. An index of materials filed;

2. Link with other information sources in Iraq and abroad to deepen cooperation and coordination;

3. Respond to requests for information from those interested in jurisprudence, legislation and adjudication;

4. Creating a secure and reliable body of information to protect the Iraqi legal legacy.

The Judicial Authority Website branch must be managed by a graduate with experience in IT and at least fifteen years legal and judicial experience, and will have a number of staff to manage daily and special requirements.

The Judicial Authority website is updated daily at http://www.iraqja.iq/ As of January 2014, the website had over 500,000 visits. The HJC's investment in staff development and IT over the past decade have resulted in sophisticated updates to previous communication tools. The website's re-design was completed by HJC staff and included:

1. An update to the site's main screen and web site design;

2. The website was re-coded to PHP language to modernize its features and allow for future evolution;

3. The addition of new fields, including one in which all Iraqi constitutions are published starting from the Fundamental Law of the Othmani government and ending with 2005 Constitution;

4. The publication of legal research and studies, including those completed by Iraqi judges and HJC staff, are published in the Research and Studies and Articles sections;

5. Statistical data on seasonal and annual court activities are posted in coordination with the Planning and Statistics Department;

6. Links have been added to connect users to the websites of other legal authorities and Arab Ministries of Justice (note that no other Arab country currently has an independent judicial branch like Iraq's);

7. A new section has been established for the Federal Supreme Court, which includes three sub-fields:

   a. Decisions related to constitutional challenges

   b. Decisions of the Federal Supreme Court in its review capacity over Administrative Court rulings

   c. Interpretive rulings on constitutional provisions

On the instructions of the President of the HJC, new website replaced older editions started under the HJC and migrated to the new Iraqi Domain (iq). The site contains the above enhancements, but maintains its old links.

CHAPTER TWELVE

Judicial Offices Overlooked by the 2005 Constitution

Section A. Judicial Training Institute (Ministry of Justice)

Judges have been selected according to standards established under judicial legal and regulatory provisions since Iraq was separated from the Ottoman Empire in the early 20th Century. This foundation remained in place even after the sovereign state of Iraq was established, and the Judicial Organization Laws of 1929 and 1945 continued to require that judges be appointed only if they met specific requirements. While demanding, this system created a highly specialized and sophisticated body of jurists.

The Judicial Service Law of 1956 amended the requirements for judicial office by increasing the length of time a candidate needed to practice law before becoming a judge to eight years from the previous minimum of three years. However, the Judicial Service Law of 1963 did not bring any further updates to the requirements.

The administration of justice remains one of the most critical state duties. Citizens must feel safe in their rights in order to participate fully in society. Developing judges in an appropriate manner creates a sound base for justice as the judges will have the technical skills and professional linkages that will allow them to live up to the demands that society asks of them. Since the Iraqi judiciary represents the essential authority in restituting violated rights, the judiciary desperately needs experienced judges armed with integrity, independence, impartiality and courage in addition to having the capacity to develop and achieve the higher goal, which is justice that everyone is seeking.

The Judicial Institute Law, Law No. 33 of 1976, established an institute to provide judges and prosecutors with the fundamental skills needed to generate fair and correct sentences and build trust through their professional service. Prior to 1976, judge and prosecutors relied on ad hoc training programs. The Judicial Training Institute (JTI) established under the Minister of Justice in 1976 created a new practical approach that built on best practices in professional development and focused on practical skills. The JTI's goal has been to qualify and train judicial candidates practically and scientifically, to develop legal knowledge and foster a legal culture based on well-founded judicial principles, and to build a judiciary capable of comprehending its role in constructing the new Iraq. The JTI maintains a system of constant review to ensure that its selection criteria and criteria reflect the social and economic changes in Iraq. There are also training programs for staff working in legal departments in various government offices.

The Judicial Training Institute Law No. 33 of 1976 stipulated:

Article one: An institute is to be established in the Ministry of Justice, to be called "the Judicial Training Institute," beholden to the MOJ and aiming to prepare qualified employees to assume judicial positions such as judges and public prosecutors, upgrade the skills of staff of the MOJ, prepare candidates for positions in the MOJ, and upgrade the legal knowledge of those who work in the legal departments of government and quasi-government institutions.

Article two: The Institute is supervised by a council called the "Institute Council." This council consists of:

First: The Chief Justice of the Cassation Court or one of his Deputies, President of the Council

Second: The head of State Consultative Council, Member of the Council

Third: The head of the Judicial Oversight Commission, Member of the Council

Fourth: The head of the Public Prosecution, Member of the Council

Fifth: The Chief Justice of Baghdad Appellate Court, Member of the Council

Sixth: The Director General of the Legal Department, Member of the Council

Seventh: The Director General of Judicial Institute, Member of the Council and Reporter

Although the Judicial Institute endeavors to provide well-trained, capable new judges to the HJC, all new judges and prosecutors benefit from practical guidance from senior members of the profession once they take up their new positions. As the institution that administers and supervises the judiciary, the HJC is responsible for selecting candidates and qualifying them as judges and public prosecutors; the HJC also gives new judges the practical training that is tailored to different responsibilities and types of courts. The JTI began as a resource of the Ministry of Justice since the judiciary were managed by the executive when the JTI was conceived. Now that the judicial authority has matured to the stage of being established independently in the 2005 Constitution, the JTI should be rejoined to the authority responsible for the judiciary. Rejoining the statutory training institute for new judges with the constitutionally mandated authority for the judicial administration will fertilize a new level of judicial and staff development. With the legal mandate to also train executive legal departments, moving the JTI to the HJC may also create new bridges between the different branches.

Section B. State Consultative Council

After the British occupation of Basrah and then Baghdad in the second decade of the 20ᵗʰ Century, the British military administration started issuing pieces of a new legal framework in the form of statements, orders, regulations and laws. The status of legislation remained like this until the Declaration handing powers over to the national government of Iraq was issued on 16 July 1921. From that point forward, every ministry in the Iraqi government drafted its own laws before sending them to the Council of Ministers to approve them prior to being debated and passed as legislation.

In 1927, an office in the MOJ was established to review drafts of laws. In practice, however, this office was quickly overwhelmed and contradicting and inaccurate laws continued to be issued. After a period of review, there was agreement that a council dedicated to legal drafting needed to be established in order to better coordinate the quality of new legislation and provide the Iraqi ministries with timely advice. Therefore, the government decided to establish a duly empowered office to draft legislation and make fatwas. The Law of the Legislation Drafting Council, Law No. 49 of 1933 was issued and published in issue #1280 of the Iraqi Gazette in 1933. The law defined the jurisdiction of the Legislation Drafting Council as preparing and organizing drafts of laws and regulations, providing legal consultation on treaties and conventions, and interpreting legal provisions and other material on request. The advice and decisions of the Council were consultative and non-obligatory, yet compliance was encouraged by the government of the day. The quality and coordination of legislation improved significantly with the input of the new Council, yet over time some weaknesses in the system became more defined. Over the years several amendments were made to the 1933 law, but the body remained a very august source of legislation and juridical review, with many of the most famous legal minds in Iraq serving as members. Some of the judges who served on the Council were:

- Justice Hameed Saeed Khudhair.

- Justice Abdul Razzaq Mubarek

- Justice Muhammad Amin Kammoona

- Justice Dhia'a sheet Khattab

The 1933 Law contained 13 Articles outlining the new Legislation Drafting Council and its duties. The First Article required the government to form the Council by stating that "[t]he Drafting Council shall consist of a president and at least four legal drafters; the Council is beholden to the Ministry of Justice." The Second Article defined the qualifications required of members of the Council, such as a good knowledge of Arabic language. The Third Article outlined the Council's jurisdiction and functions as follows:

1. Prepare and organize laws and regulations pertaining to judicial affairs and other matters concerning the offices of the MOJ;

2. Revise laws and regulations pertaining to other ministries except those of customs and duties;

3. Provide advice on contracts, treaties, and conventions made with a natural or juristic person or state whenever the government deems consultation with the Council is necessary in this regard;

4. Provide opinion and consultation on legal disputes and transactions between two or more ministries if a ministry is reluctant to apply a legal provision;

5. Interpret legal provisions at the request of a ministry;

6. Consider the legality of orders and decisions issued by staff, administrative boards and municipalities, including the capital municipality council, provided that:

   a. It is not a complaint or a lawsuit before courts;

   b. The order or decision must not be subject to a formal legal challenge;

   c. The order or decision must not be related to fees or taxes of any kind.

The Sixth Article granted the Council jurisdiction over the State Employees' Disciplinary Law No. 41 of 1929, while the Ninth Article confirmed the Council's organizational structure. As a result, the Drafting Council was divided into three divisions based on classes of activities:

1. Legislation Drafting Division,

2. Consultation Division,

3. Trial Division.

The law allowed one or more Divisions to be headed by a legal draftsman. The Drafting Council was also to provide drafting assistance to other divisions when necessary. In contrast to the later 1979 law, the 1933 law did not stipulate the formation of a general assembly made up of all drafters; however, it did allow the participation of all council members in discussing subjects referred by the President. In such a case a decision would be arrived at through discussion and a voting process and the majority opinion provided to the President. The president has the right to decide which opinion to accept in cases where the votes are equal.

In 1979, the State Consultative Council was established by Law No. 65 of 1979 and by its operation the State Consultative Council was formed to replace the Legislation Drafting Council. The legal task set for this council was intimidating, with the Law referencing the "great changes in the political, economic and social life" facing the new Council. The government of the day clearly saw the need for a more rigorous and solid legal foundation to address contemporary issues. For this reason the new State Consultative Council was formed with very senior judges and jurists as members, and their work contributed to building sound legislative foundations whose impact is still felt. The members of the new Council contributed to preparing sophisticated studies and draft bills, as well as reviewing queries from the Council of Ministers and interpreting provisions, orders and laws for other government offices. The Council also reviewed past legislation and issued a definitive collection of laws and regulation covering the period from 1917 to 1979.

Specific provisions of the 1979 law included efforts to accommodate the need for young staff to be developed through lose interaction with senior jurists, and to appropriately support the professionals called into service at the required level. Other provisions included measures establishing the General Assembly, where complicated and important issues could be freely debated by experts. The original law and subsequent amendments provided that:

First. State Consultative Council consists of Council President and his two deputies and a number of Consultants whose numbers shall not be less than twelve while the number of the Consultant assistants shall not exceed the half the number of the Consultants.

The Council shall consist of:

A. A General Assembly which is composed of the President and his deputies and consultants. Consultant assistants attend the deliberations of the Council but do not have the right to vote;

B. The Presidency which consists of the President and his deputies and heads of specialized committees;

C. An Expanded Commission which consists of two specialized committees assigned by the President;

D. A number of specialized committees each of which shall consist of a chair, who is a consultant, and a number of consultants and consultant assistants provided that their percentage shall not exceed a third of the number of Consultants;

E. State Employee Disciplinary Council;

F. Court of Administrative Justice.

Second. The jurisdiction of the State Consultative Council

The Council is responsible for:

1. Drafting Legislation

   A. Drafting laws, regulations and instructions;

   B. Revising law proposals, regulations and instructions required by higher authorities, ministries and the agencies not beholden to a ministry;

2. Providing legal opinion and consultations

   A. Providing legal opinions on conventions and international agreements;

   B. Arbitrating in disputes which arise between two or more ministries on the interpretation of legal provisions;

C. Providing legal opinion on issues submitted by higher authorities, ministries and agencies that are not connected to a ministry;

D. Requesting the clarification from bodies mentioned above in a specific topic or issue;

E. Providing legal opinion or clarification on a specific topic or issue as requested by the Minister of Justice about specific topic.

3. The Administrative Judiciary which includes

A. State Employee Disciplinary Council: this Council reviews lawsuits filed by the employees of ministries against the ministries and agencies which are not beholden to a ministry relating to the decisions issued by government and public sector offices; all issues relating to the rights arising from civil service law or other service regulations; and disciplinary penalties imposed on an employee in accordance with the provisions of the Disciplinary Law of State and public sector employees No. 14 of 1991.

B. The Administrative Court: the Court reviews the legality of orders and administrative decisions issued by government employees and commissions or other public sector bodies which have no direct legislated path for appeal.

C. General Assembly which specializes in looking into decisions issued by State Employee Disciplinary Council in its capacity as a cassation court.

Because of the high caliber of the professionals attracted to the Council and the respect that developed in the ministries and government agencies for the Council's work, the government continued to increase the demands on the Council. For this reason it was necessary to increase the number of employees, however the sophistication of the work required made it very difficult to increase the size quickly. In reality, the size of the Council has decreased in recent years.

Functions of the Council

1. Legislation Drafting

    A. The Council shall prepare and formulate draft legislation for ministries; the Council may also draft legislation for departments not subordinate to a ministry upon the request of the competent minister, or the top manager of the body that is not beholden to a ministry, once the requesting body submits the basis for the required legislation with all the supporting papers and records of the views of relevant ministries and the parties concerned.

    B. The Council checks on all draft legislations set by ministries or bodies which are not beholden to a ministry from the point view of form and subject. The Council shall study the draft and reformulate the draft where appropriate and propose alternatives it deems necessary. The Council submits the draft with recommendations to the higher authorities.

    C. The Council contributes to ensuring uniformity of wording in legislation and seeks the standardization of legal terms used in legislative drafting.

    D. The Presidency Council submits a report every six months (or whenever it deems necessary) to the Council of Ministers. The report includes information on provisions reviewed or research on legislation since the last report, noting areas of ambiguity in current legislation, cases of abuse of power by any of the administrative parties or agencies, or cases in which those authorities exceed their powers.

2. Providing Opinions and Legal Advice

First: The Council shall provide opinions and legal advice as follows:

A. When requested by higher authorities;

B. On international agreements and conventions before they are ratified or entered into;

C. Opinions will be offered on disputes between ministries, or between a ministry and a body unconnected to a ministry at the discretion of the Council. If the parties refer their dispute to the Council, the decision shall be binding;

D. If a ministry, or a party not beholden to a ministry, is reluctant to accept a legal provision, the Council shall express an opinion on the matter after the legal office of the ministry or the party concerned requests legal advice on specific issues and gives reasons for doing so. The decision of the Council is binding the ministry or the party concerned;

E. To clarify legal provisions at the request of a ministry or a body not beholden to a ministry.

Second: No case shall be heard unless the Council is requested to engage with it by a relevant minister or top manager of a body not beholden to a ministry.

Third: The General Assembly of the State Consultative Council in its Appellate Capacity:

The General Assembly of the State Consultative Council assumes the jurisdiction of the Federal Cassation Court as stipulated in the Civil Procedure Law when looking into challenges against a decision of the State Employee Disciplinary Council.

Fourth: The Council shall refrain from giving a legal opinion or advice in cases already referred to a court, or on issues where there is already a legal reference.

Fifth: The Minister of Justice can refer to the Council any case he thinks appropriate or ask one or more members of the council to study an issue and give a formal opinion. The Minister can also ask the Council to draft laws on any issue referred to it.

3. Administrative Justice

During its first several decades as a sovereign nation Iraq did not have a court authorized to hear cases challenging administrative orders or decisions of administrative commissions and officials. There was a growing awareness amongst judges, academics, and citizens that a venue was needed for citizens or others impacted by administrative action to resolve allegations of abuse of power, mis-application of regulation, or any other reason supporting a challenge. This venue would both ensure that government functionaries were acting in accordance with their authorities and also increase the trust of the people in government. The civil courts could hear some administrative cases under their general jurisdiction, however limited court resources would necessarily limit the number of cases that the courts could address. Court procedural demands also made their use expensive and time consuming, so many potential claimants would be discouraged from pursuing their rights through the civil courts. An administrative court is usually characterized by its flexibility and, in many cases, by legal discretion and ability to use regulatory precedents to resolve cases. In light of these considerations, an administrative court was established in Iraq by Law No. 106 of 1989, the Second Amendment to the State Consultative Council Law No. 65 of 1979. Article 7 of the 1979 State Consultative Council Law was amended to add a new jurisdiction which covered administrative matters in two fields:

1: Cases of State Employees: the State Employees Disciplinary Council (Disciplinary Council) moved under the State Consultative Council

The State Consultative Council was tasked to take over the moribund State Employees Disciplinary Council using a new structure. The Disciplinary Council deals with disputes arising under civil service laws covering government employees, including Article 58 of the Civil Service Law No. 24 of, which empowers aggrieved employees to file cases with the Disciplinary Council. The Disciplinary Council also looks into challenges filed by an employee against a disciplinary order imposed by a supervisor as defined by Article 15 of the State Employees Disciplinary Law No. 14 of 1991.

The State Consultative Council convenes the State Employee Disciplinary Council under the chairmanship of the President of the State Consultative Council, a Deputy to the President, or a member of the State Consultative Council. Two additional members of the Council's Board must join the Disciplinary Council sitting. Article 7/First/B of the State Consultative Council Law allows commissioning a first or second grade judge to be a member of the State Employee Disciplinary Council, however currently the Disciplinary Council is chaired by one of the consultants at the State Consultative Council. Membership is completed with consultants or assistant consultants. The Disciplinary Council reports to the State Consultative Council and has its headquarters in Baghdad as stipulated by law. Judgments and decisions of the Disciplinary Council are subject to challenge by either of the litigants before a plenary session of the State Consultative Council. Decisions are considered final if they are not challenged after the Disciplinary Council session, or on completion of the challenge to the State Consultative Council. When the State Consultative Council is hearing a challenge to a Disciplinary Council decision it acts like the Cassation Court.

2:   General Administrative Court

Article 7/Second of the Law of the State Consultative Council was amended to mandate the Council to establish an Administrative Court with a general jurisdiction. The Administrative Court is chaired by a grade one judge or a consultant in the State Consultative Council, and sits with either two additional judges whose grade should not be lower than grade two, or consultant assistants from within the Council. Since its establishment in 1989, the Court has been chaired by a first grade judge. The law stipulated that the first Administrative Court should be located within the State Consultative Council, but also allowed setting up similar courts in the District Courts on an order from the Minister of Justice. So far, only the Baghdad-based Administrative Court has been established in the State Consultative Council. It is not clear how the 1989 law would operate to establish new courts given the 2003 and 2005 expansion of the judicial branch.

the legality of administrative orders and decisions taken by employees and committees in government offices in areas where laws do not create a specific path for appeal. Those fearing harm from an order or decision must first file a formal grievance with the office responsible for the order or decision in question. There is no time limit imposed on the complainant, but the law stipulates that the office responsible for the order or decision must respond to the filed grievance within 30 days from the date it is filed. If the grievance is rejected, or if it is not responded to within 30 days, the complainant has the right to lodge a challenge to the order or decision with the Administrative Court. The challenge must be filed by the complainant within 60 days of either the rejection or the expiration of the 30 day window for the office's response. This time period is strictly enforced. Any complaint not filed within the time frame will be dismissed and the right to challenge the order or decision is lost.

The Law lists the following non-exclusive list of possible grounds for challenging an order or decision:

1. The order or decision may violate a law, regulation or instruction;

2. The order or decision may have been issued in violation of the rules of specialization directing that duly authorized bodies issue orders or decisions in their narrowly defined area of specialization, or there could be a flaw in the form of the order or decision;

3. The order or decision is based on a mistake in the implementation of a law, regulation or instruction, an abuse of power on the part of the issuing office, or a challenge could be filed if the competent office or employee refrains from issuing a decision or an order that should be issues.

The Administrative Court is barred from addressing challenges to:

1. Acts of sovereignty, including decrees and decisions issued by the President;

2. Administrative decisions made in according with the directions of the President within that office's area of constitutional competence;

3. Administrative decisions subject to legally established avenues for challenging that do not include the Administrative Court.

Administrative Court Procedures

The Administrative Court reviews a filed challenge to see if: 1) it is lodged within the specified time period; 2) it was filed as a grievance first with the relevant office making the questioned order or decision (or which should have made a requested order or decision); and 3) the challenge falls within the Court jurisdiction without having a separate route in law for appeal. With regard to the third point, Article 7/Fourth of the State Consultative Law stipulates how to resolve a dispute between a First Instance Court and Administrative Court over which body has jurisdiction over a challenge. The law mandates that a joint committee be formed of Cassation Court judges and members of the State Consultative Council to resolve the issue. Challenges that meet these criteria will be assessed by the Administrative Court. The Court will either reject the challenge if it has no legal basis or accept the challenge by repealing or amending the administrative order or decision. In such a case, the Court will also consider restitution for the complainant if it has been requested in accordance with the law.

Prior to March 17, 2005 challenges against the Administrative Court sentence or order were heard at the General Assembly of the State Consultative Council according to provisions of Article 7/Second of the State Consultative Council Law. This caused great embarrassment especially to the first grade chief justices of the Court since it placed their sentences and orders under review by civilian employees rather than higher grade judges. The civilian employees were all very senior, however they did not have the legal training or experience to appropriately review the complex issues presented in cases. Moreover, the bureaucratic hierarchy requires the civilian employees to continue to report to their executive superiors, so this system made it impossible to ensure the neutrality in effect as well as appearance. Complainants would always question whether a minister's employee would be neutral when hearing their challenge. Article Third/4 of the Federal Supreme Court Law No. 30 of 2005 addressed this shortcoming by stating that appeals of Administrative Court decisions should be made to the Federal Supreme Court instead of to the General Assembly.

Comment

The formation of the Administrative Court in 1989 was a step forward on the way to establish a court specialized in looking into challenges against the decisions and orders of executive authorities. The state of Iraq was strengthened by creating an avenue for citizens to hold government accountable for decisions that could be abuses of power, or be based on the misinterpretation of a law, regulation or instructions. Unfortunately, the Administrative Court emerged weakly due to the limitations of the system at the time. The Administrative Court was formed as a means to repeal or amend executive power decisions if they cause grievance or result from misinterpretation rather than as a true, independent oversight body.

The Administrative Court should not come under the control of the executive power. Referring to the Administrative Court Law No. 106 of 1989, we find that the Administrative Court is a component of the State Consultative Council, which is itself a component of the Ministry of Justice and reports to the Minister. However well-intentioned the Minister of Justice may be, it is unfair to ask that office leave aside its fundamental duty to further the aims of the executive authority, and it is unfair to ask citizens to trust that the executive agency is able to act as a neutral arbiter. How can we, then, resort to the executive power when we are in dispute with it?

How can we believe in a court's impartiality in a case involving the executive if it later reports to that executive power?

Many of these issues were in fact considerations leading to the drafting of Article 47 of the 2005 Constitution of the Republic of Iraq creating a distinct judicial authority. Since the provisions establishing the Administrative Court and the Government Employees' Disciplinary Council were drafted 15 years before the new Constitution, it should be expected that there would be some areas of friction. In simple fact, the 1989 structure within the Ministry of Justice clearly violates the spirit and intent of the 2005 Constitution.

Looking beyond the potential injustice at the level of review allowed to date, it is critical to note that the 1989 law also severely constrained the ability of the Administrative Court to review challenges made against decisions related to the highest executive office, that of the President of the Republic. Other limitations, such as the failure to allow extensions of the State Employee Disciplinary Council outside of Baghdad, are surely a source of inconvenience, if not a denial of access to justice, to employees posted outside of the capital.

Heads of the State Consultative Council

No.	Name	Date	
		From	To
1.	Judge Fakhri Midhat	11/7/ 1979	16/12/1980
2.	Dr. Abdul Abdul Rasool al—Jasani	17/12/1980	14/4/1984
3.	Judge Akram Abdul al-Qader Ali	15/4/ 1984	17/1/1988
4.	Dr.Ali Hussain al-Khalaf	8/1/1988	25/6/ 1989
5.	Judge Abul Majeed Salman al-Janabi	26/6/1989	24/9/1991

6.	Mr. Adnan Abud Ahmad	**25/9/1991**	**2/8/2000**
7.	Judge Madhat al-Mahmood	**3/8/2000**	**23/8/2004**
8.	Dr. Qais Abdul Satar Authman	**24/5/2004**	**23/1/2007**
9.	Asmat Abdul Majeed Baker	**24/1/2007**	**1/4/2007**
10.	Mr. Gazi Abraheem al-Janabi	**13/5/2007**	**Present**

Section C. The Court Order Implementation Office

The Court Order Implementation Office, at times called the "Order Execution Office", takes up the task of giving the right to its appropriate owner once there is either a consensual agreement or a court order confirming the rightful owner.

This role is well established in Iraq, and there have been specialized offices established to support the enforcement of orders throughout Iraq's modern history. For example, during the Ottoman period there was a Procedural Offices that implemented orders under the Ottoman Procedural Law issued on 5/Shawal/1288 A.H. (approximately 1870 A.D.). Under the British occupation, the Procedural Offices remained open and applied the Ottoman Law within the 1917 directives issued by British authorities. Under the Ottoman Law, the Procedural Offices only enforced court judgments so a party could not file a negotiated agreement, regular bond, or commercial document for enforcement until the Ottoman law was amended around 1913. In 1945, the Court Establishment Law No. 3 was issued, and the Order Implementation Office (Implementation Office) was established to replace the Procedural Offices.

Following the passage of the 1945 law, the Ministry of Justice formed an Implementation Office wherever a First Instance Court was established. The Implementation Office was headed by a judge; in many locations, this judge would also be responsible for the affiliated First Instance Court so people commonly linked the court process with the enforcement process. A senior clerk and other support staff typically supported the judge with Implementation Office efforts.

Changing circumstances required updates to the resources available for the Implementation Office to ensure the timely, fair enforcement of agreements and orders. The Implementation Law No. 30 of 1957 included new legal and procedural protections for citizens, such as:

1. The 1957 law confirmed that the procedures of the Implementation Office were themselves part of the public law framework and no private agreement could contravene them. This provision protected individuals from signing away their right access to the support of the Implementation Office by accident or through manipulation.

2. The law introduced measures to restrict the sale of debtor's property.

3. The law confirmed the linkage of the Implementation Office to the First Instance Court, and, thereby, to the District Court that managed the First Instance Court.

Despite the issuance of this law, its procedures remained the same as promulgated under the Ottoman law dating back to around 1870. Both the creditors and the debtors suffered from dealing with this system. Protections for both had increased through successive revisions to the law, yet the procedures for claiming rights or protecting interests remained lengthy and complex since they were rooted in 19th Century tools and systems. By all accounts, the Implementation Office remained the most backward of all the Ministry of Justice systems at the time.

Law No. 35 of 1980 addressed some of the most egregious problems faced by citizens attempting to implement court orders and other agreements. The law established a central office to effect the reorganization of the Court Order Implementation Office within the Ministry of Justice. The law created a Director General position to head the new Implementation Office, mandating that the Director General have at least a bachelor's degree in law and at least 12 years of judicial or legal experience. In addition, the law authorized a first or second grade judge as the manager of the reorganized office. Within the 1980 law, the Implementation Office and related procedures were intended to:

1. Maintain the right of the state to keep order;

2. Make procedures for enforcing court orders, private agreements, and commercial documents more accessible and efficient;

3. Maintain the rights of citizens;

4. Improve trust and reliance on laws and the in the government;

5. Improve the awareness of citizens on resources available to them for enforcing court orders or other instruments.

The first judge to fill the position of Director General of the reformed Implementation Office was Justice Midhat Al—Mohmood, who held the post until Dec 7.1985 and is currently the Chief Justice of the Federal Supreme Court. The most recent Director General of this office is Mr. Hadi Mahdi Abdul Hussain, who has filled this position since April 1, 2004.

Court Order Implementation Office Statistics

- Number of Court Order Implementation Offices: 121

- Number of court order implementers: 65

- Total number of employees: 592

- Number of directorates run by the court order implementers: 44

- Number of directorates run by judges: 47

Section D. The Office of the Notary Public

In 1296 A.H. (approximately 1874 A.D.), the Ottomans created a position of "contract editor", which is similar to a notary public, to provide services throughout the empire, including Iraq. Prior to the creation of this law, an Ottoman law from 1839 required judges in the personal status courts to provide ratification services in support of various transactions.

In 1913, the Ottoman Government issued the Temporary Notary Law. In line with the earlier revisions of the criminal code fostered by Ottoman strategies to modernize their systems to become more competitive with western European economic powers, the new notary law also strongly resembled similar laws from France, Switzerland and Austria. By virtue of this law, the task of ratification was assigned to the new notary position instead of the personal status judges. It seemed that this law was applied in Mosul before it was applied in Baghdad because many of the notary records were found in Mosul are dated to era before 1323 A.H. (approximately 1905 A.D.). While many records were lost during the flight of the Ottomans after 1914 that could create gaps in archives at some locations, there are other reports that confirm that the first notary did not begin work in Baghdad until 1917 under the British occupation.

The historic notary records contain a wealth of different transactions, such as sales, leases, long-term cultivation agreements; records of disputes over irrigation, wills, endowments, confirmations of lineage and plans for distribution of estates, orchard leases, and government revenue collection contracts. Most of these were written in Arabic, while some were written in both English and Turkish with Arabic translations. Although the notary position was created by law, the position itself did not have any definite job description. In practice, the work of notaries overlapped with the jurisdiction of courts and of the Real Estate Registration Office. Three laws later clarified the obligations of notaries:

- Law No. 35 of 1938;

- Law No. 31 of 1939, covering the registration of machinery, and later amended by Law No. 56 of 1952, the Registration of Equipment Regulation No. 65 of 1952, and Regulation No. 27 of 1953, which amended Regulation No. 65;

- The Notary Regulation No. 21 of 1940.

Domestic and international transactions continued to increase in number and complexity through the middle of the 20th Century and the old notary laws were not able to address societal demands. The Notary Law No. 27 of 1977 amalgamated the Registration of Equipment Regulations and related amendments, but did not make other fundamental changes. Finally, Law No. 33 of 1998 was issued to better organize the obligations and jurisdiction of notaries and their offices. According to this Law, the jurisdictions have been identified as follows:

1. The organization and the documentation of described legal instruments and transactions, with the exclusion of those covered by special legal provisions, including those related to the operation of the Trade Law, the Law on the Rental of Real Estate, and the Law of Commercial Brokerage;

2. Endorsing translations after obtaining the oath of a translator on the authenticity of his / her translation;

3. Confirming the financial competence of a sponsor;

4. Receiving cash deposits, deposits in kind, and securities in support of agreements, transactions or orders;

Notary offices developed procedures to effect the efficient and accurate implementation of the 1998 law. The law created enough flexibility for notaries to adapt to manage new technologies and advances in photocopying, new forms of various commercial transactions, and other services used to process transactions in in large numbers. By 2011, there were 142 Notary Offices, of which 35 were run by judges and 107 were managed by Notaries.

Section E. Minors' Assets Management Department

In Iraq, assets of minors that were wards of the state were run according to the Ottoman Orphan's Assets Management Regulations issued in 1333 A.H. (approximately 1914 A.D.). In 1934 Iraqi Law of Inheritance Distribution and Orphan Assets Management replaced the Ottoman law. Assets of minors were managed under this law until the 1969 Minor Assets Management Law No. 47 was passed.

The 1969 law was notably weak and offered little advancement over the 1934 law other than the establishment of the a General Directorate for the Assets of Minors. In practice, the interests of minors were subjugated to the interests of government employees that gained access to favorable loans made against the collected assets of the minors. Little effort was recorded by government actors to perform custodial functions obligated by the law. This situation sadly expanded to the point that the Departments of Minors Assets around the country became more like financial institutions. Lending was eventually limited to only real estate transactions through the Al—Rafidain Bank, and Departments of Minors Assets were prohibited from lending. Other primarily financial reforms to the 1969 law and related procedures were also implemented. Amongst other areas, these reforms:

- Addressed the financial status of Minors Asset Management Departments in Baghdad and the terminated suspended accounts;

- Created regulations to require certificates of descent and distribution certificates be issued to parents and guardians to better protect the interests and rights of minors;

- Organized procedures for making distributions or payments;

- Required the production of a guide on the management of minors' assets;

- Enhanced other linkages between the Minors Assets Management Departments and the custodians and guardians to better protect the interest of minors and create paths to address issues through the courts.

Despite these efforts within the framework of the 1969 law, however, further progress against objectives was not possible without new legislation. In 1980 the Minors' Assets Management Law No. 78 was issued with the following new elements:

- All minors and those who are equivalent, i.e. people with certain disabilities, must be assigned to a Minors' Assets Management Department;

- New mechanisms established to improve coordination between competent courts and Minors' Assets Management Department;

- New structures within the Departments established to meet new and existing obligations;

- Procedures for the Departments to monitor and replace guardians and custodians in the interest of the minor;

- Increased flexibility to allow the Departments to respond to advances provided through on-going Sociological Research. To support this shift, new methods of maintaining files on minors were developed;

- Higher priority on maintaining and growing the assets of the minors to provide greater benefits to the minors.

- A new council was formed to give full effect to the provisions of the 1980 law. Chaired by the Minister of Justice, the council also included a number of specialists from the Ministry of Justice, other ministries and concerned authorities. The council was tasked to develop plans to improve the care of minors, enhance the efficiency of the MoJ's related Directorates, and monitor the implementation of the law and related plans by issuing instructions to assist responsible parties.

- A new Minors Care Directorate was formed with a well-qualified Director General to manage the activities of the Minor's Care offices established in all provinces and local government offices around the country.

- A new Board of Custodians and Guardians was formed to ensure cooperation between the Directorates and the custodians and guardians of minors. The Board was also intended to support healthy linkages within families.

The law focused on financial matters both to address previous problems and in light of the importance of creating a stable platform of support for the minors. The law created a special Minor's Care Fund within the Department funds provided by returns from Minor's Care Board deposits in the Minor's Assets fund, from bequests or residual amounts from those passing away without known descendants or a will in place, from allocations within the state Budget, and, finally, from grants and other financial assistance.

Monthly payments are made for the care of the minor from the Minors Care Fund to the Minors Care Department, which tops up the funds for care if the minor is out of resources and there is no family to sponsor him until he reaches puberty. The Fund is also available to pay emergency costs for minors on application.

Over the decades the Department and its subsidiaries have evolved under the guidance of the two councils. Today, specialist staff create strategies to meet the long term need of minors based on the latest social research, and approaches include field and home visits to assess home situations with guardians and review challenges faced by the minors. There are dedicated social workers in the system now looking after the minor's health and social, academic, educational, and family conditions. As noted above, the 1980 law created a mechanism for the Department to file cases protecting the minor, and obligated the Department to notify the public prosecutor if criminal behavior is suspected. As a result of the upgraded General Directorate, several well-respected judges assumed control of the Directorate over the years. These included: Judge Yousif Al–Ma'mar, Judge Madhat Al Mahmood, and Judge Fadal Hamid Al Khateeb.

Section F. Real Estate Registration Office

The first office in Iraq responsible for registering real estate transactions was formed in Baghdad by the Ottomans in 1287 A.H. (approximately 1870 A.D.) under the name of the Directorate of Ottoman Sultanate Records. There were also sub-offices established in smaller administrative centers throughout Baghdad governorate. The Baghdad offices were all empowered to issue deeds, a major improvement over the former system of needing to wait for a deed to be issued by the Directorate of Ottoman Sultanate Records in Astana (the former name of Istanbul). Directorates were later formed along similar lines by the Ottomans in the governorates of Mosul and Basrah. Initially, the Directorate of Ottoman Sultanate Records was limited to the registration of transactions relating to the sale of state-owned land or the transfer of land in the event of a death, in which case the transfer was completed by permission of the officer in charge of the Directorate in the location of the property. Then the jurisdiction of these offices was expanded to include the endowed land with existing buildings and real estate owned by individuals.

Following the establishment of the Iraqi State, a Land Registry Office was legislated, later to be reorganized into the Real Estate Registration Office. In addition, a Land Registry General Directorate was formed in Baghdad to coordinate the formation and operation of the sub-offices in governorates and in local administrative centers. While the names of the offices changed, the work of the offices and Directorate remained largely the same as under the Ottoman legislation. Records produced during this period were considered presumptive evidence of rights to a property. The records also served to protect mortgage interests until the passage of the Law of Assets Registration for Real Estate in the Land Registry, Law No. 59 of 1935. Although Regulation No. 64 of 1959 was passed, the need for greater protections of rights in real estate disposition became clear. Law No. 43 of 1971 provided additional procedures for the sale and registration of real estate that gave additional protection to parties. The Law provided that no real estate transactions were binding unless they were recorded in the land register. There were also additional safeguards to ensure the accuracy of the land register itself, including linkage to an audit committee and other measures.

In 1981 an extensive Amendment to the Real Estate Registration Law No. 181 required the registration of all real estate in Iraq. A second amendment in 182, Law No. 31 of 1982, provided more clear regulations on procedures and structures covering real estate registration and sale.

Some of the more prominent Director Generals of the Real Estate Registration Office have been: Mr. Abdulaziz Al-Hassani, Mr. Younis Al Musslih, Mr. Abdullah Ghazai, Mr. Zidane Khalaf, Mr. Kaduem Bedin, and Mr. Adel Mustafa.

PART 4

A Personal Note on the Constellation of Martyrs Created Through the Sacrifice of Iraqi Judges, Court Staff, and Families

The judiciary has been targeted by terrorist organizations and criminal groups. Judges were a symbol of justice and the hope of people during the difficult times in Iraq's history. They remain a symbol of these rights rising in partnership with the people and providing a national symbol to all struggling to build the state of law in the new Iraq. No one takes the path to being a judge lightly, and, sadly, sacrifices have long been part of the judicial spirit. Those that have given the lives so that the rest of us can retain our hope for the future continue to contribute as symbols of how important our endeavor to build a new state is. They inspire us to work yet harder to create a state, constitution, laws, and regulations that befit Iraqis and our history. So now we think of these precious and cherished sacrifices that have joined the long martyr's caravan made of Iraq's filial stars.

It also obvious that the terrorists and criminal groups have dedicated themselves to schemes to attack the dedicated, immaculate figures that have gone. Each judge sits upon a family's lifetime of investment and a personal commitment that cannot be measured. While the souls of the fallen judges are still flying in the sky of Iraq they illuminate the dream of all of us Iraqis: a country of bothers united under the rule of law; a home where all are equal regardless of their religion or doctrine, free no matter how different their race, their thoughts and their social status may be from others in the great family. Iraqis can still taste this dream on our lips although it has been missing for so very long.

We weep for our lost colleagues who have fallen because the judiciary stands on behalf of the people that want the rights promised in the Constitution. The Iraqi judiciary still adheres to its independence and neutrality; still does not meddle in politics; and still disassociates itself from political blocs and warring groups. No matter how many attacks we must face, we are committed to the independence granted to us by the people so that we may contribute to building the rule of law under a universally applied constitution, side by side with the legislative and executive authorities.

Hope for a revived Iraq is linked to the emergence of faith in the values of justice. People can start to see that progress in Iraq is linked to a shared compliance with the legal system so that all can have faith in their rights within the constitution. The political and social progress in Iraq is measured by how strong, neutral, and reliable the judiciary is. Judges play an essential role in extending the umbrella of constitutional rights to all the corners of the country, places that previously suffered greatly from the political storms.

In view of this important role in building a new state open to all nestled under the constitution, the judiciary is targeted by those possessed by the demons of terror and crime.

Those many brilliant figures that died in service to Iraq remain examples of attitudes, decisions, and character that will show us all the road forward. Their bodies are gone, as all of ours will be one day, but their souls are still among us still watching with joy as we continue the work of building the new Iraq.

The list below gives names of martyred judges through 2011 according to the date of their martyrdom. May all rest in peace.

Name	Position	Date of Martyrdom
Aqeel Ibrahim Qasir Al Ani	Karbala Investigative Judge	17 June 2003
Ismael Yousif Sadiq	Deputy President of Ninawa Appellate Court	4 November 2003
Mohan Jabir Zarzoor Al Shuwaili	President of Al Najaf Appellate Court	13 November 2003
Yousif Khorshid Gha'eb	Al Mosul Investigative Judge	23 December 2003
Abdul Ameer Hussein Nahim Al Robai'ee	Al Hilla Investigative Judge	20 March 2004

Abdul Ameer Kadhum Jabor	Member of Wasit Criminal Court	14 October 2004
Qais Hashim Muhammad Bandar Al Shimmary	Secretary General of the Higher Judicial Council.	2 January 2005
Salim Mahmood Ali Abdul Kareem	Mosul Misdemeanor Judge.	16 June 2005
Noor Aldin Ahmed Dawood Al Diwan	Al Nasiriya Misdemeanor Court	15 July 2005
Taha Yaseen Hussein Al Ameer	Deputy President of Al Basra Appellate Court	July 2005
Jasim Muhammad Abid Al Fraji	Al Door First Instance Court	8 September 2005
Jasim Wahab Dwiach Bidan	Al Karkhh Investigative Judge	8 September 2005
Mustafa Kadhum Abbood Al Mudamgha	Member of the Federal Cassation Court	1 December 2005
Khalid Hazza'a Rasheed Najim	Kirkuk Investigative Judge	9 January 2006
Ibrahim Malik Al Hindawi	Judge of Al Bayaa First Instance Court	5 April 2006
Haitham Ali Abbas Nsaief	Judge	4 May 2006
Muhaimin Mahmood Abbood	Al Adhamiya First Instance Court	10 May 2006
Akram Jima'a Abid Muhammad Al Ma'amoory	Personal Status Judge, Al Karkh.	21 May 2006
Mohammad Shakir Mahmood	Al Karkh Office of the Public Prosecutor	19 July 2006
Turkey Zabin Armit	Tikrit Investigative Judge.	17 August 2006
Naeem Hassan Salman Al Ogaili	Deputy President of Al Karkh Appellate Court	2 November 2006

Tariq Abid Ali Al Qaisi	Office of the Public Prosecutor, Dyala.	2 November 2006
Mohammad Zain Al Abideen Mahdi	Office of the Public Prosecutor, Diyala	20 January 2007
Omar Abdul Nabi Abdul Hussein Abbas	Al Karrada Investigative Judge	13 March 2007
Asa'ad Jabbar Ibrahim Al Juboori	Deputy Chief Justice of Diyalla Appellate Court	29 April 2007
Saleem Jasim Mahmood Jawad Al Din	Personal Status Judge, Al Adhamiya.	3 June 2007
Haqqi Ismael Abbood	Al Miqdadia Investigative Judge	9 July 2007
Hamdi Habib Jasim	Al Khalis Investigative Judge	16 July 2007
Ahmed Jasim Mohammad	Office of the Public Prosecutor, Diyalla	1 August 2007
Adnan Ali Juwyyier	Deputy Chief Justice, Al Karkh Appellate Court.	26 August 2007
Aqeel Adnan Hassoon Witwit	Personal Status Judge, Al Adhamiya.	2 September 2007
Salah Abbas Hassan Hussein	Al Karrada Investigative Judge	24 November 2007
Amir Jawdat Al Na'ib	Member of Federal Cassation Court	14 January 2008
Abid Jasim Hanash	Investigative Judge of the Juvenile Delinquency Court in Nineva	29 February 2008
Munaf Mahdi Salih	Personal Status Judge in Tikrit	25 March 2008
Qasim Ali Mutar	Investigative Judge, Abu Ghraib.	22 May 2008

Kamil Abdul Majeed Al Showaili	President of Al Rusafa Appellate Court	26 June 2008
Mohammad Khalaf Sabeel Salih	Deputy Chief Justice, Nineva Appellate Court	31 July 2008
Hashim Rasheed Hassoon	Office of the Public Prosecutor, Babylon	29 December 2008
Abbas Jussein Hassan Ahmed	Tall'afar Investigative Judge	16 October 2009
Ahmed Barud Kumar	Public Prosecutor, Karrada Misdemeanor Court	18 January 2011
Mohammed Abdul Gafur Azzez Al-Khafa	Office of the Public Prosecutor, Rusafa	16 March 2011
Tumaa Jabbar Lafta	Al-Karkh Investigative Judge	30 April 2011
Talib Mahmud Abbass Al-Azzawi	Tikrit Personal Status Court Judge	3 June 2011
Hassan Azzez Abdul Rahman Al-Alaaf	Judge, Federal Cassation Court	14 July 2011
Najim Abdul Wahid Jala Al-Talibani	Judge, Federal Cassation Court	17 August 2010
Bassim Tahir Kumar	Al-Bayaa Personal Status Court Judge	9 June 2011

The family members of judges also face constant threats as the terrorists desperately attempt to subvert justice through attacks against even the most innocent. The martyrs lighting our way to a better future include family members of judges and the inspirational employees of courts from around the great nation. Some of the staff martyred in support of justice and a new Iraq are:

1. Ali Aziz Kadhum – 16/6/2004. Babylon Appellate Court.

2. Muhammad Muhammad Saeed Qadir – 21/6/2004. Al Qaem First Instance Court.

3. Abdul Wahab Habeeb Abbas – 11/11/2004. Baghdad – Al karkh Appellate Court.

4. Jasim Adnan Abdullah – 6/12/2004. Baghdad – Al karkh Appellate Court.

5. Hani Mahdi Abo Al Ma'ali – 15/5/2005. Baghdad – Al karkh Appellate Court.

6. Muhammad Mutar Tlaab – 2/3/2006. Al Habbaniya First Instance Court.

7. Kamal Rasheed Muhammad – 2/5/2006. Baghdad/Al Risafa Appellate Court.

8. Firas Kadhum Sadiq – 11/5/2006. CCCI/ Al Karkh.

9. Salahiddin Kareem Abbas – 18/7/2006. Baghdad/Al Risafa Appellate Court.

10. Aryan Mirdan Sadiq – 26/7/2006. Kirkuk Investigative Court.

11. Sabbar Bresam Ayesh 29/7/2006. Diyala A ppellate Court.

12. Abdullah Hasson Elaiwi – 22/9/2006. Salahiddin Appellate Court.

13. Arkan Abdul Wahab Abdullah – 29/9/2006. Al Madaen Court.

14. Naseer To'ma Muhammad – 4/10/2006. Baghdad/ Al Karkh Appellat Court.

15. Finjan Munaf Geetan – 12/10/2006. Dyala Appellate Court.

16. Hassan Hussein Hadi – 3/12/2006. Dyala Appellate Court.

17. Muhammad Ahmed Ali – 25/1/2007. Baghdad/Al Karkh Appellate Court.

18. Taha Ali Jabir – 2/2/2007. Babylon Appellate Court.

19. Yaseen Taha Yaseen – 5/3/2007. Al Adhamyah Investigatine Court.

20. Hashim Abdullah Breesam – 25/3/2007. Public Prosecutor Office in Diyalla.

21. Assaf Hussan Iddin Assaf – 7/4/2007. Al Basra Appellate Court.

22. Moayed Kadhum Madhloom – 8/4/2007. Al Mithana Appellate Court.

23. Sattar Salman Sha'lan – 7/6/2007. Babylon Appellate Court.

24. Asa'ad Hammoody Wasmi – 15/7/2007. Baghdad/Al Karkh Appellate Court.

25. Ra'ad Rasheed Fayadh – 5/8/2007. Justice Court in Al Madaen.

26. Sami Attallah Ali – 11/9/2007. Salahidin Appellate Court.

27. Qasim Abdullah Shihab – 15/9/2007. Diyalla Appellate Court.

28. Zuhair Ni'ema Salman – 25/10/2009. MoJ HQ Bombing.

29. Eman Siham Hamid – 25/10/2009. MoJ HQ Bombing.

30. Saif Zaki Hadi – 25/10/2009. MoJ HQ Bombing.

31. Tahqiq Muhammad Hamza – 25/10/2009. MoJ HQ Bombing.

32. Muhammad Ibrahim Khaleel – 25/10/2009. MoJ HQ Bombing.

33. Abbas Sadiq Ja'afar – 25/10/2009. MoJ HQ Bombing.

34. Ara Karabet Hanna – 25/10/2009. MoJ HQ Bombing.

35. Samir Matty Na'oom – 25/10/2009. MoJ HQ Bombing.

36. Ahmed Dhia'a Kammas – 8/12/2009. Cassation Court Bombing.

37. Ahmed Waleed Najim – 8/12/2009. Cassation Court Bombing..

38. Majid Hussein Ali – 8/12/2009. Cassation Court Bombing..

Every one of those people represents a treasure of knowledge, an investment of the nation, and a distinctive mind that is impossible to value. Terrorists and criminals realize that the loss of a judge or experienced staff member is a wound to the nation of Iraq; it is their aim to impoverish Iraq from the loss of its children, its faithful men and women, and undermine the values that make Iraq proud amongst nations.

Great names have been engraved on the wall of justice in Iraq; let the wall become a bastion to protect our future efforts. The souls of our lost colleagues have left our world, and their absence in the legal field is felt every day. The judiciary is keeping these prominent names and their bright and honest history engraved in our minds. The courts desperately needed each of them. Their prodigious service brought us through the storms, and it is on their efforts that we will march forward in building the new state of law.

The judges of Iraq have risen to the challenge of a federal democratic Iraq, and proudly stand as the cornerstone of the nation. We stand against terrorism and criminal groups and refuse to bow to the terrorists trying to push Iraqis back to a state of fear, submission, and dictatorship; we draw our swords to confront the murderers, thieves and criminals.

These martyred judges, in addition to their distinctiveness in the judicial field, filled our world with poetry, writing and research. These judges braved terrorism armed only with the word of right, the shield of justice and protected by the providence of Allah, saying fearlessly the word of truth, knowing they will meet God Who will ask them about the decisions and judgments they issued. At that moment, the criminals will realize that they stood against the will of God on earth since the judges, begging support from Allah to extract themselves from their own minds and desires, dipped into the realm of Allah to do His bidding, deriving a small amount of his wide justice towards human beings to provide the light of justice in this world as was their mission. While judges work, there will always be people dedicated to His Justice. Terrorism uses fear, darkness and chains to enslave people with lies. The truth brought by judges as a tool of Allah is poison to the lies, which is why judges remain a target of evil. Many judges and members of their families have been subjected to cowardly and mean attempts to hurt them in order to pervert the course of justice, to silence them so that they do not share the word of truth, to feed the appetite of the oppressors.

Today, while we recall some of these names with reverence and respect, we feel they and their families have the right to be proud of their monumental service and sacrifice. We whisper to them our gratitude, and acknowledge the high standards that they have set for all of us still here toiling. They are the lamps that illuminate the way to all those who work in the lofty and formidable HJC courts, those who sacrificed themselves without wavering in lifting us all towards a new society glowing with democracy, federalism and the rule of law.

APPENDICES

Chief Justice with Senior Judges,
Najaf District Court—2011

COALITION PROVISIONAL AUTHORITY ORDER NUMBER 35[132]

Re-Establishment of the Council of Judges

Pursuant to my authority as Administrator of the Coalition Provisional Authority (CPA), and consistent with relevant U.N. Security Council resolutions, including Resolution 1483 (2003), and the laws and usages of war

Noting that, prior to the changes made by the former regime, Iraq had a functioning Council of Judges that administered the judicial and prosecutorial systems to insure that judges and public prosecutors were appointed from among persons enjoying the highest reputation for fairness and integrity and of recognized competence of law, and that the judicial system exercised its authority in accordance with the rule of law, and

Recognizing that a key to the establishment of the rule of law is a judicial system staffed by capable persons and free and independent from outside influences

I hereby promulgate the following:

---

[132] CPA/ORD/13 SEP 2003/35.

Section 1

Purpose

This Order establishes the Council of Judges ("the Council"), which is charged with the supervision of the judicial systems of Iraq. The Council shall perform its functions independently of the Ministry of Justice.

Section 2

Membership

The following officials shall serve as members of the Council:

- Chief Justice of the Cassation Court (President of the Council)

- The Deputy Chief Justices of the Cassation Court

- Director-General of the State Consultative Council

- Director-General, Legal Oversight Office

- Director-General, Administration, if such person is a Judge or Prosecutor

- Chief Justices of the Appellate Courts

- The Council shall also have a Secretary-General, who shall be selected by the President of the Council. The Secretary-General shall perform administrative functions for the Council, together with such additional employees as the Council may deem appropriate.

Section 3

Duties (Amended)

The Council shall have the following specific duties:

A. To provide administrative oversight of all the judges and all public prosecutors, excluding, however, the members of the Cassation Court.

B. To investigate allegations of professional misconduct of judges and public prosecutors, and, when appropriate, to take appropriate disciplinary measures against them, including termination from the office.

C. To nominate and recommend qualified persons, as required, filling judicial or public prosecution vacancies.

D. To promote, increase yearly salary, loan, transfer and delegate judges and prosecutors.

E. To assign judges and prosecutors to hold specific judicial and public prosecutor posts as provided for in the Law of Judicial Organization (Law No. 160 (1979)) and the Law of Public Prosecution Law No. 159 of (1979))

F. The Council shall have such other duties as may be determined from time to time by law.

Section 4

Meetings

1. The Council shall conduct regular meetings at least monthly. The President may recall the Council when needed

2. A quorum shall require at least three-fourths of the members of the Council with the presence of either the President or the Vice-President of the Council. Decisions of the Council will be by majority vote of those members present.

Section 5

Disciplinary Committee

1. The Council shall appoint a Disciplinary Committee of at least three (3) members from its own membership. The Committee shall investigate allegations of misconduct by members of the judiciary and public prosecutors, and shall make appropriate decisions concerning disposition of those allegations, including but not limited to, the removal of that judge or prosecutor from office if the allegations are substantiated.

2. Any judge or prosecutor adversely affected by a decision of the Committee may appeal the decision to the Council within thirty (30) days from the date of the decision of the Committee. The decision of the Council on the appeal shall be final and conclusive, and no further appeal against the decision is authorized.

Section 6

Independence of the Council

1. The Council shall perform its duties and responsibilities independently of any control, oversight, or supervision by the Ministry of Justice. To the extent that provisions of Iraqi law, specifically the Law of Judicial Organization (Law No. 160 (1979) and the Law of Public Prosecution (Law No. 159) (1979» conflict with the provisions of this Order, those provisions of Iraqi law are suspended.

2. The Council of Judges shall replace the Council of Justice in its jurisdiction that was previously established by the Judicial Organization Law (Law No. 160) (1979) as far as the Council of Justice exercised any authority over any judge or prosecutor. All administrative oversight of the judges and prosecutors shall now rest only with the Council of Judges. The Council of Justice shall continue in existence, but shall have no jurisdiction over any prosecutor or judge.

Section 7

Entry into Force

This Order shall enter into force on the date of signature.

19 August 2003

L. Paul Bremer,

Administrator, Coalition Provisional Authority

COALITION PROVISIONAL AUTHORITY MEMORANDUM NUMBER 12[133]

ADMINISTRATION OF INDEPENDENT JUDICIARY

Pursuant to my authority as Administrator of the Coalition Provisional Authority (CPA), and under the laws and usages of war, and consistent with relevant U.N. Security Council resolutions, including Resolutions 1483 and 1511 (2003), *Recognizing* that an independent judiciary as provided for in CPA Order No. 35 and the Law of Administration for the State of Iraq for the Transitional Period requires an independent judicial administration.

Recognizing further that Iraqi law still reflects the lack of an independent judiciary which was one fundamentally malign feature of the former regime that undermined the rule of law,

I hereby promulgate the following:

---

[133] CPA/MEM/8 May 2004/12.

Purpose

Article 1

This Memorandum implements CPA Order No. 35 and Chapter six of the Law of

Administration for the State of Iraq for the Transitional period

Definition

Article 2

For purposes of this regulation, "Council of Judges" means the Council of Judges reestablished by CPA Order 35, or its successor organization as provided by the Law of Administration for the State of Iraq for the Transitional Period

Budget

Article 3

The Council of Judges and the Court of Cassation shall each have its own, separate budget by no later than June 1, 2004. The Ministry of Finance shall cooperate fully to create, fund, and support each such budget, including reallocating money from the budget of the Ministry of Justice as appropriate. For the year 2004, the Ministry of Finance shall determine, in consultation with the Ministry of Justice, the Council of Judges, and the Court of Cassation, the amount of the budget of the Ministry of Justice for 2004 that shall be reallocated to the latter two entities, and shall attempt to minimize any additional 2004 budget expenditures concerning these two entities.

Personnel

Article 4

All employees who work for or are primarily associated with the courts, including but not limited to all judges, prosecutors, court investigators, court clerks, personnel on the Committee of Judicial Oversight, security personnel, and support and administrative staff, and are currently employed by the Ministry of Justice, shall, no later than June 1, 2004, become employees of the Council of Judges or of the Court of Cassation, as appropriate.

Property

Article 5

All interests in property, real, tangible, or otherwise, including but not limited to furniture, motor vehicles, office equipment, libraries, and housing for judges and prosecutors, that is primarily used for or associated with courts and the judiciary and that is assigned to the Ministry of Justice, shall, no later than June 1, 2004, be assigned to the Council of Judges or to the Court of Cassation, as appropriate.

State Consultative Council

Article 6

The State Consultative Council shall remain a part of the Ministry of Justice.

References in Law

Article 7

References in Iraqi law to the Ministry of Justice or the Minister of Justice shall, here necessary and proper in light of CPA Order 35 or the Law of Administration for the State of Iraq for the Transitional Period, or where otherwise necessary and proper to maintain the independence of the judiciary, be construed to refer to the Council of Judges or its President, or to the Court of Cassation or its Chief Judge, or to the Federal Supreme Court or its Presiding Judge, as appropriate. The courts shall have sole jurisdiction to adjudicated disputes in this connection

Article 8

Cooperation

The Ministry of Justice, the Council of Judges, the Court of the Cassation, the Ministry of Finance, and all other concerned government institutions shall cooperate to execute what this memorandum and the CPA Order No. 35 stipulate.

Article 9

Implementation

This Order shall enter into force on the date of signature.

L. Paul Bremer,

Administrator, Coalition Provisional Authority

LAW OF ADMINISTRATION FOR THE STATE OF IRAQ FOR THE TRANSITIONAL PERIOD[134]

– Selected Sections—

Chapter Six

The Federal Judicial Authority

Article 43

A. The judiciary is independent, and it shall in no way be administered by the executive authority, including the Ministry of Justice. The judiciary shall enjoy exclusive competence to determine the innocence or guilt of the accused pursuant to law, without interference from the legislative or executive authorities.

B. All judges sitting in their respective courts as of 1 July 2004 will continue in office thereafter, unless removed from office pursuant to this Law.

---

[134] http://www.refworld.org/docid/45263d612.html   [Editor's Note: the official CPA site posting documents from this period is no longer maintained so an actively managed site was selected for reference].

C. The National Assembly shall draw up an independent and adequate budget for the judiciary.

D. Federal courts shall adjudicate matters that arise from the application of federal laws. The establishment of these courts shall be within the exclusive competence of the federal government. The establishment of these courts in the regions shall be in consultation with the presidents of the judicial councils in the regions, and priority in appointing or transferring judges to these courts shall be given to judges residing in the region.

Article 44

A. A court called the Supreme Federal Court shall be constituted by law in Iraq.

B. The jurisdiction of the Supreme Federal Court shall be as follows:

1. Original and exclusive jurisdiction in legal proceedings between the Iraqi Transitional Government and the regional governments, governorate and municipal administrations, and local administrations.

2. Original and exclusive jurisdiction, on the basis of a complaint from a claimant or a referral from another court, to review claims that a law, regulation, or directive issued by the federal or regional governments, the governorate or municipal administrations, or local administrations is inconsistent with this Law.

3. Ordinary appellate jurisdiction of the Supreme Federal Court shall be defined by federal law.

C. Should the Supreme Federal Court rule that a challenged law, regulation, directive, or measure is inconsistent with this Law, it shall be deemed null and void.

D. The Supreme Federal Court shall create and publish regulations regarding the procedures required to file claims and to permit attorneys to practice before it. It shall take its decisions by simple majority, except decisions with regard to the proceedings stipulated in Article 44(B)(1), which must be by a two-thirds majority. Decisions shall be binding. The Court shall have full powers to enforce its decisions, including the power to issue judgment for contempt of court and the measures that flow from this.

E. The Supreme Federal Court shall consist of nine members. The Higher Juridical Council shall, in consultation with the regional judicial councils, initially nominate no less than eighteen and up to twenty-seven individuals to fill the initial vacancies in the aforementioned Court. It will follow the same procedure thereafter, nominating three members for each subsequent vacancy that occurs by reason of death, resignation, or removal. The Presidency Council shall appoint the members of this Court and name one of them as its Presiding Judge. In the event an appointment is rejected, the Higher Juridical Council shall nominate a new group of three candidates.

Article 45

A Higher Juridical Council shall be established and assume the role of the Council of Judges. The Higher Juridical Council shall supervise the federal judiciary and shall administer its budget. This Council shall be composed of the Presiding Judge of the Supreme Federal

Court, the presiding judge and deputy presiding judges of the federal Court of Cassation, the presiding judges of the federal Courts of Appeal, and the presiding judge and two deputy presiding judges of each regional court of cassation. The Presiding Judge of the Federal Supreme Court shall preside over the Higher Juridical Council. In his absence, the presiding judge of the federal Court of Cassation shall preside over the Council.

Article 46

A. The federal Judicial Authority shall include existing courts outside the Kurdistan region, including courts of first instance; the Central Criminal Court of Iraq; Courts of Appeal; and the Court of Cassation, which shall be the court of last resort except as provided in Article 44 of this Law. Additional federal courts may be established by law. The appointment of judges for these courts shall be made by the Higher Juridical Council. This Law preserves the qualifications necessary for the appointment of judges, as defined by law.

B. The decisions of regional and local courts, including the courts of the Kurdistan region, shall be final, but shall be subject to review by the federal judiciary if they conflict with this Law or any federal law. Procedures for such review shall be defined by law.

Article 47

No judge or member of the Higher Juridical Council may be removed unless he is convicted of a crime involving moral turpitude or corruption or suffers permanent incapacity. Removal shall be on the recommendation of the Higher Juridical Council, by a decision of the Council of Ministers, and with the approval of the Presidency Council. Removal shall be executed immediately after issuance of this approval. A judge who has been accused of such a crime as cited above shall be suspended from his work in the judiciary until such time as the case arising from what is cited in this Article is adjudicated. No judge may have his salary reduced or suspended for any reason during his period of service.

2005 CONSTITUTION – JUDICIAL PROVISIONS

Constitution of the Republic of Iraq, Articles (87 – 94)

Judiciary

Article 87:

The Judicial authority is independent. The courts, in their various types and classes, shall assume this authority and issue decisions in accordance with the law.

Article 88:

Judges are independent and there is no authority over them except that of the law. No authority shall have the right to interfere in the Judiciary and the affairs of Justice.

Article 89:

The Federal Judicial Authority is comprised of the Higher Juridical Council, Supreme Federal Court, Federal Court of Cassation, Public Prosecution Department, Judiciary Oversight Commission and other federal courts that are regulated in accordance with the law.

FIRST: Higher Juridical Council

Article 90:

The Higher Juridical Council shall oversee the affairs of the Judicial Committees. The law shall specify the method of its establishment, its authorities, and the rules of its operation.

Article 91:

The Higher Juridical Council shall exercise the following authorities:

First: To manage the affairs of the Judiciary and supervise the Federal Judiciary.

Second: To nominate the Chief Justice and members of the Federal Court of Cassation, the Chief Public Prosecutor, the Chief Justice of the Judiciary Oversight Commission and present them to the Council of Representatives to approve their appointment.

Third: To propose the draft of the annual budget of the Federal Judiciary Authority and present it to the Council of Representatives for approval.

SECOND: Federal Supreme Court

Article 92:

First: The Federal Supreme Court is an independent judicial body, financially and administratively.

Second: The Federal Supreme Court shall be made up of a number of judges, and experts in Islamic jurisprudence and law experts whose number, the method of their selection and the work of the court shall be determined by a law enacted by a two-third majority of the members of the Council of Representatives.

Article 93:

The Federal Supreme Court shall have jurisdiction over the following:

First: Oversight of the constitutionality of laws and regulations in effect.

Second: Interpretation of the provisions of the constitution.

Third: Settle matters that arise from the application of the federal laws, decisions, regulations, instructions, and procedures issued by the federal authority. The law shall guarantee the right of each of the Cabinet, the concerned individuals and others of direct contest with the Court.

Fourth: Settle disputes that arise between the federal government and the governments of the regions and governorates, municipalities, and local administrations.

Fifth: Settle disputes that arise between the governments of the regions and governments of the governorates.

Sixth: Settle accusations directed against the President, the Prime Minister and the Ministers. That shall be regulated by law.

Seventh: Ratify the final results of the general elections for membership in the Council of Representatives.

Eight:

A. Settle competency dispute between the Federal Judiciary and the judicial institutions of the regions and governorates that are not organized in a region.

B. Settle competency dispute between judicial institutions of the regions or governorates that are not organized in a region.

Article 94:

Decisions of the Federal Supreme Court are final and binding for all authorities.

ADDITIONAL RESOURCES

al Anbari, Abdul Razak. *The Judicial System in Baghdad During the Abbasid Period*. al Najef: al Numa'an Press, 1977.

al Anbari. *Chief Justices in the Abbasid Period*. Beirut: Arab House for Encyclopedias, 1987.

al Arab, Lisan. *Arab Tongue*. Beirut: Dar Sadir Publishers, 1994.

al Asoutty, Dr. Tharwat Anees. "Committed Judiciary and Revolutionary Legitimacy." *Judiciary Journal*, no. 1 (1938).

al Humaeidy, Abdulrahman Ibraheem. *The Judiciary and Court Systems in the Quran and the Teachings of Mohammed*. Mecca: Um al Qura University Press, 1409 AH.

al Kayai, Ahmed Zaki. *A History of Law Practice in Iraq*. Baghdad, 1947.

al Mahmood, Madhat. *Interpretation and Practical Applications of the Civil Procedure Law, No. 183 of 1969*. Baghdad: al Husam Company, 1994.

al Ukeily, Professor Abdul Ameer, and Dr. Saleem Harbah. *Interpretation of Criminal Procedure Law*, vol. 1. Baghdad: Pub. Unk., Year Unk.

al Wafa, Ahmed Abu. *Civil and Commercial Procedure*, 5th Ed. Cairo: Pub. Unk, 1956.

Allam, Abad al Rahman. *Principles of Iraqi Procedural Law*. City Unk: Pub. Unk., Year Unk.

Alyian, Dr. Shawkat. *Grievance Judgment*. Riyadh: Dar Al Rasheed Publishers, 1980.

Arsalaan, Mohammed Shaheer. "Judiciary and Judges." *Al Arabee Magazine* (1962).

Arsalan, Mohammed Shaheer. *Judiciary and Judges*. Riyadh: King Fahad National Press, 1969.

Arslan, Mohammed Shaheer. *Judges and the Judiciary*. Riyadh: King Saud Press, 1969.

Asfoor, Dr. Mohammed Asfoor. *Independence of the Judicial Branch*. Cairo: Pub. Unk., 1968.

Ashmawee, Mohammed, and Abdul Wahab al Ashmawee, *The Rules of Hearings in Egyptian Legislation*, vol. 1, 2nd ed. Cairo: al Namuthajiyyah Press, Year Unk.

Farj, Ismael Haqi. *The History of the Islamic Judiciary*. City Unknown: Ibraheem al-Wa'ad, 1949.

Kubah, Abulhameed. *Judicial Organizations and Legislative Trends in Iraq*. Baghdad: Pub. Unk, Year Unk.

Kudir, Abdulrahman. "Judicial Development in Iraq." *Judiciary Journal*, no. 1 (1937).

Ministry of Justice. "Process and Achievement" (1984).

Qura 'al Kareem

Saif, Dr. Ramzi. *Interpretation of Civil and Commercial Procedures*, 2nd ed. Kuwait City: Kuwait University Press, 1974.

Surur, Dr. Ahmad Fathi. *The Interpretation of the Criminal Procedure Law*, vol. 1, 4th ed. Cairo: Dar al Nahda al Arabia Publishing House, 1981.

Yagi, Ismael Ahmed. *Ottoman Empire in Modern Islamic History*. City Unknown: Alabeekan Bookshop, 1996.

A BRIEF NOTE ON JUSTICE MADHAT AL—MAHMOOD

Chief Justice Madhat Al-Mahmood—Date Unknown

Chief Justice of Higher Judicial Council – Chief Justice of Federal Court

1. Assigned as Judicial Investigator in the Ministry of Justice 1960

2. Assigned as a Judge in many Iraqi courts among which the courts of Qalah Sukar, Al Refaee, Hindyia Barrage, Al Moseib, Al Ramadi Juvenile Court in Baghdad, Al Kadumiah Court of First Instance, and Baghdad Court of First Instance.

3. Seconded from the judiciary to be Director General of the Court Implementation Order Office he established in 1980.

4. Seconded from judiciary to be Director General of Minors Directorate.

5. Assigned as Deputy Chief Justice of Baghdad Appellate Court, Chief of Civil Cassation Commission.

6. Assigned as consultant in the State Consultative Council while retaining his judicial capacity; assigned as Chief Justice of Administrative Court. Later assigned as Chief of State Consultative Council.

7. Assigned as a judge in the Cassation Court through unanimous vote of the General Commission of Cassation Court.

8. Assigned as Supervisor of Ministry of Justice on 12 June 2003.

9. Assigned as Deputy Chief Justice of Cassation Court.

10. Assigned as Chief Justice of Cassation Court.

11. Assigned as Chief Justice of Federal Supreme Court in March 30, 2005. He still retains this position, in addition to the presidency to the HJC which was established in Sept 18, 2003.

12. An Arab Expert in the field of Civil and Personal Status Laws, Arab League.

13. Visiting Professor in Civil Procedures Law and Implantation Law, and Laws of Judicial Organization, for 26 years in the Judicial Institute.

14. Participated in many regional and international conferences.

15. Supervised tens of legal researches.

16. Many of his judicial researches were published in Arab Journals.

17. Authored the following books:

A. Interpretation of Implementation Law.

B. Interpretation of Civil Procedures Law. (1st Part)

C. Interpretation of Civil Procedures Law (2nd Part)

D. Interpretation of Civil Procedures Law (3rd Part).

E. Judiciary in Iraq (3 Editions).

18. A founding member of the Arab Center of Legal and Judicial Studies.

19. A member in Arab Center of Development the Rule of Law and Integrity.

EDITOR'S EPILOGUE

I came across an early version of a section of this book, which was produced for a UNDP conference, around 2009 while working in Iraq for the Department of State. Several years later, I learned that the section had been incorporated into a larger book and published by Chief Justice Madhat in Arabic. After realizing that both Arab Spring and Iraq transition discussions could benefit greatly from the insights of the Chief Justice, Abubakr Zaid and I obtained the permission of the Chief Justice to produce this English edition in 2011.

This First English Edition provides additional information and citations on historical or legal elements that we learned were unfamiliar to Western readers. My apologies to the Chief Justice for the long delay in producing this edition, and for the errors that remain in capturing the technical elements and tone of the original. I thank colleagues that helped in the review of several issues from a Western perspective over the years, especially Forde Fairchild and Sherizaan Minwalla, so that the translation could be as accessible as possible.

In the historical review starting this book, the Chief Justice reports that the growth of the courts was interspersed with periods where some Ottoman and British actors sought to contain or side-step the courts in the interest of political priorities. While the British supported the extension of justice services when they assumed control of Iraq in the early 20th Century, their representatives tended to come from police or military perspectives that considered court processes a necessary evil rather than a critical part of a healthy process. They also failed to integrate their new systems and laws with the civil law systems introduced by the Ottomans while struggling with the demands of WWI.

Perhaps with an understanding of the confusion created by British missteps, but more likely in furtherance of the dominant state-building ideology of the times, in 2003 the US pronounced the establishment of an independent judiciary as a political priority in its own right by issuing a CPA Order to re-establish an independent administrative body for the courts.

Unfortunately, some of the winds blowing in Basrah in 1914 were also blowing in Baghdad after 2003 and momentum for strengthening non-police and security actors waned. By 2008, military and police actors were the predominate international voices in the security and justice sectors due to both numbers and resources. As a result, and with good intentions in many cases, military and police courts were established to operate independently from civilian courts in areas of overlapping jurisdiction, decades of forensics capacity developed in the Ministry of Health was abandoned in favor of laboratory capacity within the police themselves, short-cuts around criminal procedure rules, including detention periods, were supported by elements of the international community in the interest of expediting some version of justice, and only a handful of laws, such as the one discussed by the Chief Justice in the Addendum and those establishing military and police courts, navigated the massive backlog crippling Parliament.

Rather than being a clear priority, the newly independent judicial branch was seen as an impediment by some with short term objectives or was considered a luxury to be sorted through later. For over a decade some international and domestic representatives favored executive bodies or military institutions at the expense of the judicial and legislative branches, which still require a number of resources just to meet mandatory functions outlined in the 2005 Constitution.

At the same time, a handful of efforts did emerge to support the constitutionally mandated civilian court structures. The Chief Justice discusses some of the work of INL, and important contributions from UNDP, the EU, the US Department of Justice, the US Commerce Department and others all added to the measured growth of court capacity. These contributions were not enough to bridge the gaps in governance initiatives, however, and the courts and legislative elements within Iraq are still not always positioned to provide balance to the historically all-powerful executive.

By outlining the history, achievements, and remaining challenges for courts in Iraq, the Chief Justice issues a quiet rallying call for a shared recommitment to finally establish and resource the equal branches required by the 2005 Constitution. This message still appears timely for both Iraq and the other nascent democracies in the Middle East since stability will remain elusive without branches capable of providing checks and balances to each other.

William Pryor
December 5, 2013
Nairobi